ISRAEL TRAVEL GUIDE 2023

The Ultimate Travel Guide to Exploring the Top Destinations, Essential Encounters, and Best-Kept Secrets in Israel.

By Maxwell Macron

Table of Contents

Jerusalem

..... It was a chilly morning in March when I landed at Ben Gurion Airport, my heart was racing with anticipation. Although I had read Maxwell Macron's Israel Travel Guide but I still felt a bit apprehensive about what lay ahead.

Israel is a country of contrasts and contradictions, where the past and present converge in the strangest ways. I had always wanted to travel there. And now, finally, after months of planning and getting ready, I was here.

I couldn't help but be in awe of the busy masses and the strange sights and sounds as

I exited the plane and made my way through the airport. Everything was so brand-new and thrilling, from the Hebrew signage to the aroma of falafel and hummus to the vibrantly colored scarves and kippahs.

As soon as I stepped outdoors into the brilliant sunshine, I was awestruck by the beauty of the surroundings. It was unlike anything I had ever seen before: the undulating hills, the golden meadows, the distant sea, and the glittering blue sky.

Jerusalem, the capital of Israel, was my first trip. For thousands of years, followers of all three of the world's major religions have revered this city. I was astounded by the labyrinth of tiny lanes and winding pathways inside the Old City's centuries-old walls, where the sounds of prayer and music blended with the aromas of spices and incense.

I went to the Western Wall, which is the holiest place in Judaism and where people go to pray and find comfort. I was in awe of the Church of the Holy Sepulchre, where Christians think Jesus was crucified and interred, and the Dome of the Rock, an Islamic shrine that glistened golden in the sunlight.

Jerusalem was more than just a metropolis of historic structures and sacred locations. The city also had lively markets and hopping neighborhoods where I could sample Middle Eastern cuisine and mix with folks from all walks of life. Jerusalem provided a complex tapestry of experiences that captivated me, from the vibrant stalls of the Mahane Yehuda market to the hip cafes of the Mamilla quarter.

I left Jerusalem and went out into the hills and valleys, where I found some of the most beautiful scenery in Israel. The Judean Hills provided a calm haven from the bustle of the city with their terraced vineyards and olive orchards. Hikers and nature enthusiasts found refuge in the Ein Gedi Natural Reserve, a desert oasis tucked between the Dead Sea and the Judaean Desert. A tribute to the tenacity and valor of the Jewish insurrectionists who resisted the might of the Roman Empire was the ancient fortress of Masada, built atop a rocky mountain overlooking the Dead Sea.

When I traveled north from Jerusalem, I came upon a place that was a tapestry of cultures and religions, each of which woven its own distinctive thread into the history of Israel. I went to the Church of the Annunciation in Nazareth, where Mary is reputed to have seen the angel Gabriel. I walked through a network of alleyways and historic citadels in Akko, which were evidence of the city's long history as a vital port city. I visited the magnificent Baha'i Gardens in Haifa, which are a UNESCO World Heritage Site and fall down a hillside with views of the Mediterranean Sea.

The city that never sleeps and the pulsating center of Israeli modern culture is Tel Aviv. Here, I discovered a thriving, multicultural city that housed some of the best eateries, museums, and cultural organizations in the entire world. Tel Aviv provided a world-class experience that was comparable to that of any other city in the globe, from the hip stores of Rothschild Boulevard to the hipster cafes of Neve Tzedek.

But Tel Aviv also had a long history, so I made care to research it as well. I went to Independence Hall, the location of David Ben Gurion's 1948 proclamation establishing the State of Israel. The city's renowned white Bauhaus buildings stood tall and high, a tribute to the city's architectural legacy, as I strolled along the lovely Mediterranean Sea beaches. And I was in awe of Jaffa, a historic port city, with its charming lanes, lively art galleries, and a port that goes back to the Bronze Age.

Yet more than just Israel's sights and noises captured my imagination. My journey was made particularly memorable by the kindness and hospitality of the people I encountered along the route, from the enthusiastic tour guides to the amiable street merchants. Everywhere I went, people greeted me with a grin and a want to tell me about their lives and how much they loved their nation.

One meeting in particular stands out in my mind: I encountered a Bedouin family in the Negev Desert. We had a lunch of freshly baked bread, goat cheese, and potent Arabic coffee inside their tent after they graciously welcomed me there. I listened in astonishment as they spoke about their customs and their passion for their culture as they described their nomadic existence and strong connection to the earth.

These kinds of experiences are what will always remind me of my journey to Israel. Although I had come to this country as a tourist, I departed as a friend with lifelong memories and experiences. And I was aware that I would always be grateful to Maxwell Macron and his Israel Travel Guide for introducing me to a world of wonders and guiding me toward understanding the beauty and diversity of this magnificent nation.

I had longing, nostalgia, and a profound sense of gratitude for the trip I had taken as I got on the plane to return home. I had fallen in love with Israel, and I knew I would come back one day to this nation of contrasts and paradoxes, where the past and present coexist in the most amazing manner.

Gambrel Roberts

CHAPTER 1: INTRODUCTION TO ISRAEL

Israel is a land of contrasts and contradictions, a place where ancient history and modern innovation collide. It is a country that has been shaped by its past, yet constantly evolves to meet the challenges of the future. From the winding streets of Jerusalem's Old City to the bustling beaches of Tel Aviv, Israel is a country that beckons visitors with its rich cultural heritage and natural beauty.

In this comprehensive Israel travel guide, we invite you to join us on a journey through this vibrant and dynamic country. We will explore its many treasures, from the ancient ruins of Masada to the vibrant nightlife of Haifa. We'll wander through the narrow alleyways of the Old City, where the scent of spices mingles with the sounds of the muezzin's call to prayer. We'll sample the flavors of the local cuisine, savoring the rich aroma of freshly baked challah bread and the tangy taste of homemade hummus.

But Israel is not just a place of historic significance and culinary delights. It is also a land of remarkable natural beauty, with sparkling blue seas, dramatic desert landscapes, and rolling green hills. We'll take you to the serene shores of the Sea of Galilee, where you can relax in the shade of a palm tree and watch the boats drift lazily by. We'll explore the rugged hills of the Negev Desert, where the silence is broken only by the gentle rustle of the wind.

As we travel through Israel, we will introduce you to its diverse people and cultures, from the devoutly religious Jews and Muslims to the secular and progressive Tel Avivians. We'll show you how the country's unique blend of old and new has created a vibrant and dynamic society, where tradition and innovation coexist in harmony.

Whether you're planning a short trip or a longer stay, this Israel travel guide will provide you with all the information you need to make the most of your visit. We'll guide you through the must-see attractions, offer insider tips on the best restaurants and cafes, and help you navigate the country's complex transportation system. So pack your bags, grab your passport, and join us on a journey through the land of Israel.

Overview of Israel's Geography, History, Culture, And Language

Israel is a small yet diverse country located in the Middle East, bordered by Lebanon to the north, Syria to the northeast, Jordan to the east, and Egypt to the southwest. Its location at the crossroads of Asia, Europe, and Africa has made it a melting pot of cultures, religions, and languages, with a rich history that spans thousands of years.

Geography

Israel's geography is as diverse as its people. The country is divided into four main regions: the Coastal Plain, the Central Mountains, the Jordan Rift Valley, and the Negev Desert. The Coastal Plain is a narrow strip of land along the Mediterranean Sea that is home to most of Israel's major cities, including Tel Aviv, Haifa, and Netanya. The Central Mountains, also known as the Judean Hills, run through the center of the country and are home to Jerusalem, Israel's capital city. The Jordan Rift Valley is a long, narrow valley that stretches from the Sea of Galilee in the north to the Red Sea in the south. The Negev Desert is a vast, arid region in the south that covers over half of Israel's land area.

History

Israel's history is as old as human civilization itself. The land that is now Israel has been inhabited by various peoples and empires throughout the centuries, including the Canaanites, the Israelites, the Assyrians, the Babylonians, the Persians, the Greeks, the Romans, the Byzantines, the Arabs, the Crusaders, the Ottomans, and the British.

The modern state of Israel was established in 1948, following the end of British rule in Palestine and the partition of the land into two states: Israel and Palestine. The establishment of Israel was a response to centuries of persecution and oppression of the Jewish people, culminating in the Holocaust during World War II. The new state of Israel was recognized by the United Nations and has since become a thriving democracy, a center of innovation and entrepreneurship, and a leader in technology, science, and culture.

Culture

Israel's culture is as diverse and vibrant as its geography. The country is home to a mix of Jewish, Muslim, Christian, and Druze communities, each with its own unique traditions and customs. Jewish culture is the dominant culture in Israel and is celebrated through food, music, dance, and art. Israeli cuisine, for example, is a fusion of Jewish, Middle Eastern, and Mediterranean flavors, with dishes such as falafel, hummus, and shakshuka being popular around the world.

Music is also an important part of Israeli culture, with a mix of traditional and modern styles that reflect the country's diverse heritage. Israeli dance is another popular art form, with traditional folk dances such as the hora and the debka being performed at weddings and other celebrations.

Language

Hebrew is the official language of Israel and is spoken by the majority of the population. Hebrew is an ancient language that was revived in the late 19th century as part of the Zionist movement to establish a Jewish homeland in Palestine. Today, Hebrew is a modern language that is spoken by over nine million people worldwide, with most of them living in Israel.

Arabic is also an official language in Israel, and it is spoken by the Arab minority in the country. English is widely spoken as a second language, particularly in business and academia, and many Israelis also speak Russian, French, and Spanish.

Tips for Travel Planning, Including When to Visit and How To Get There

Traveling to Israel can be a life-changing experience, but it requires careful planning to ensure a smooth and enjoyable trip. From deciding when to go to figuring out how to get there, there are several important considerations that can help make your trip a success.

When to Visit

The best time to visit Israel depends on your preferences and interests. Israel has a Mediterranean climate, which means that it has hot, dry summers and mild, rainy winters. The peak tourist season is during the summer months (June to August), when the weather is warm and sunny, but the crowds can be overwhelming. If you prefer a quieter experience, consider visiting during the shoulder seasons (April to May and September to October), when the weather is still pleasant, but the crowds are smaller.

Another important factor to consider when planning your trip to Israel is the Jewish calendar. Israel is a Jewish state, and many of its holidays and festivals are observed throughout the country. The High Holy Days (Rosh Hashanah and Yom Kippur), Sukkot, and Passover are all popular times to visit, but they can also be more expensive and crowded.

How to Get There

There are several ways to get to Israel, depending on your location and budget. The most common way to travel to Israel is by plane, with the major international airport located in Tel Aviv. There are several airlines that offer direct flights to Israel from major cities around the world, including New York, London, Paris, and Moscow.

Another option for traveling to Israel is by land, particularly if you are coming from neighboring countries such as Jordan or Egypt. The Allenby/King Hussein Bridge border crossing is the main entry point for travelers entering Israel from Jordan, while the Taba border crossing is the main entry point for travelers entering from Egypt.

Visa Requirements

Most visitors to Israel do not need a visa to enter the country for stays of up to 90 days. However, it is important to check the visa requirements for your specific nationality before you travel to ensure that you have all the necessary documentation.

Accommodation

Israel has a wide range of accommodation options, from luxury hotels to budget-friendly hostels. It is important to book your accommodation well in advance, particularly if you are traveling during the peak tourist season. Major cities such as Tel Aviv and Jerusalem have a wide range of options to choose from, but smaller towns and villages may have limited options.

Transportation

Israel has a well-developed transportation system, with buses, trains, and taxis available throughout the country. Buses are the most common form of public transportation and are a convenient and affordable way to get around. Trains are also available, although they are not as extensive as the bus network.

Taxis are also widely available, but they can be expensive, particularly for longer journeys. If you plan to rent a car, be aware that driving in Israel can be challenging, particularly in major cities such as Tel Aviv and Jerusalem.

Safety and Security

Israel is a safe destination for travelers, but it is important to be aware of the security situation and follow local advice. The Israeli government provides regular updates on the security situation, and it is important to stay informed if you are traveling to the country.

Planning a trip to Israel requires careful consideration of several important factors, including when to visit, how to get there, accommodation options, transportation, and safety and security. By taking the time to plan your trip carefully, you can ensure a smooth and enjoyable experience that will leave you with lasting memories of this fascinating and unique destination.

CHAPTER 2: GETTING AROUND ISRAEL

Israel has a well-developed transportation system that makes getting around the country convenient and easy. Buses are the most common form of public transportation, with both intercity and intracity routes available. Israel Railways also operates trains between major cities and towns. Taxis are widely available and can be hailed on the street or ordered in advance. Rental cars are also available for those who prefer to drive themselves. It is important to note that public transportation does not operate on the Sabbath, so be sure to plan accordingly.

Transportation Options Within Israel (e.g. Buses, Trains, Taxis, Car Rentals)

Israel is a small country, but it is rich in history and culture, with many attractions to explore. Getting around Israel is relatively easy, thanks to its well-developed transportation system. From buses and trains to taxis and car rentals, there are several options to choose from depending on your preferences and budget.

Buses

Buses are the most common form of public transportation in Israel, and they offer a convenient and affordable way to get around. There are several bus companies that operate throughout the country, including Egged and Dan, which offer both intercity and intracity routes.

Intercity buses run between major cities and towns and are generally comfortable and reliable. Many buses are equipped with air conditioning and free Wi-Fi, making the journey more comfortable. Tickets can be purchased at the bus station or on the bus itself, although it is recommended to purchase in advance to ensure a seat.

Intracity buses are also available in most cities and towns and provide an affordable way to get around. They are particularly useful for traveling to attractions within a city or town. It is important to note that some buses do not run on the Sabbath (from Friday evening until Saturday evening), so be sure to plan accordingly.

Trains

Trains are another option for getting around Israel, although the network is not as extensive as the bus network. Israel Railways operates trains between major cities and towns, including Tel Aviv, Haifa, and Jerusalem. The trains are generally clean and comfortable, and offer a scenic way to travel between destinations.

Tickets can be purchased at the train station or online in advance. It is important to note that trains do not operate on the Sabbath, so be sure to plan accordingly.

Taxis

Taxis are widely available in Israel and provide a convenient way to get around, particularly for shorter journeys. Taxis can be hailed on the street or ordered in advance by phone or through a ride-sharing app such as Gett or Uber. Taxis are metered, and it is recommended to confirm the fare with the driver before beginning the journey.

Car Rentals

If you prefer to drive yourself, car rentals are available from several companies, including Avis, Budget, and Hertz. Renting a car gives you the freedom to explore at your own pace and visit attractions that may be off the beaten path. However, driving in Israel can be challenging, particularly in cities where traffic can be heavy, and parking can be difficult to find. It is recommended to have a GPS navigation system or a map to help navigate the roads.

It is important to note that driving in Israel can be quite different from driving in other countries, particularly in terms of road rules and signage. The speed limit is generally 50 km/h in built-up areas and 90 km/h on highways, although this may vary depending on the road conditions. It is also important to note that many Israeli drivers are aggressive, so it is important to be alert and cautious on the roads.

There are several transportation options available in Israel, including buses, trains, taxis, and car rentals. Each option has its advantages and disadvantages, and the best option for you will depend on your preferences and budget. Regardless of which option you choose, be sure to plan ahead and be aware of any restrictions or limitations, particularly on the Sabbath.

Tips for Driving in Israel

Driving in Israel can be a thrilling and enjoyable experience, but it is important to be aware of the unique driving culture and road rules in the country. Here are some tips for driving in Israel:

1. Be aware of road signs and markings Road signs in Israel are written in Hebrew, Arabic, and English. It is important to pay attention to the signs and markings on the road to avoid getting lost or driving in the wrong direction. In some areas, the road signs may not be as clear, so it is recommended to have a GPS navigation system or a map to help navigate the roads.

2. Understand the speed limits The speed limit in Israel is generally 50 km/h in built-up areas and 90 km/h on highways. However, there may be variations depending on the road conditions, so it is important to pay attention to the signs. In some areas, there may be speed cameras, so be sure to adhere to the speed limit to avoid fines.

3. Be aware of aggressive driving Many Israeli drivers are known for their aggressive driving style, particularly in cities. It is important to be alert and cautious on the roads and avoid engaging in aggressive behavior. Keep a safe distance from the car in front of you and use your turn signals to indicate lane changes and turns.

4. Pay attention to parking regulations Parking in Israel can be challenging, particularly in cities where parking spaces are limited. It is important to be aware of the parking regulations, including parking times and restrictions. In some areas, parking may be restricted to residents only, so be sure to check the signs before parking.

5. Know the road conditions Israel has a diverse landscape, ranging from coastal plains to mountainous regions. The road conditions can vary depending on the area, so it is

important to be prepared for different driving conditions. In some areas, the roads may be narrow and winding, so it is important to drive carefully and stay alert.

6. Be aware of religious and cultural events Israel is a religious country, and there are several religious and cultural events that may impact driving conditions. For example, during the Sabbath, many roads are closed, and public transportation does not operate. It is important to be aware of these events and plan accordingly.

7. Consider renting a GPS navigation system If you are unfamiliar with the roads in Israel, it may be helpful to rent a GPS navigation system or use a navigation app on your phone. This will help you navigate the roads more easily and avoid getting lost.

Driving in Israel can be an enjoyable experience, but it is important to be aware of the unique driving culture and road rules in the country. By following these tips, you can ensure a safe and enjoyable driving experience in Israel.

Information About Local Airports and International Flights

Israel has several airports that serve both domestic and international flights. The main international airport is Ben Gurion Airport, located near Tel Aviv. It is the largest airport in Israel and serves as the hub for many international airlines. There are direct flights to and from many destinations around the world, including Europe, Asia, Africa, North America, and South America.

Another major airport is Eilat Ramon Airport, located in the southern city of Eilat. It primarily serves domestic flights and flights from neighboring countries, but there are also some international flights to and from Europe.

Other airports in Israel include Haifa Airport, located in the northern city of Haifa, and Ovda Airport, located in the Negev desert. These airports mainly serve domestic flights and flights from neighboring countries, but there are also some international flights to and from Europe.

When booking international flights to Israel, it is important to consider the time of year and the popularity of the destination. High season for tourism in Israel is generally from June to September, so flights during this time may be more expensive and crowded. It is recommended to book flights in advance to get the best deals and to ensure availability.

There are many airlines that operate flights to and from Israel, including national carrier El Al, as well as international carriers such as British Airways, Air France, Lufthansa, Emirates, and many others. It is recommended to compare prices and services to find the best option for your needs.

In addition to commercial flights, there are also private aviation options in Israel, such as charter flights and helicopter tours. These options may be more expensive, but they offer a unique and luxurious way to see the country from above.

Local Travel Agencies and Tour Operators

If you are planning a trip to Israel, you may want to consider using a local travel agency or tour operator. These companies offer a range of services, from booking flights and accommodation to arranging tours and activities. Here are some of the benefits of using a local travel agency or tour operator:

1. Local knowledge and expertise Local travel agencies and tour operators have a deep understanding of the local culture, customs, and geography. They can provide valuable insights and recommendations on the best places to visit, the best time to travel, and the best ways to experience the local culture. They can also help you navigate any challenges or obstacles that may arise during your trip.

2. Tailored itineraries A local travel agency or tour operator can help you create a customized itinerary that suits your interests, preferences, and budget. They can suggest activities and tours that are off the beaten path and not commonly known to tourists. This can help you have a more unique and authentic travel experience.

3. Cost savings Using a local travel agency or tour operator can often save you money, as they have access to special deals and discounts that are not available to the general public. They can also help you find the best prices on flights, accommodation, and activities.

4. Convenience and peace of mind Planning a trip can be time-consuming and stressful, particularly if you are unfamiliar with the destination. A local travel agency or tour operator can take care of all the details, from booking flights and accommodation to arranging tours and activities. This can save you time and give you peace of mind, knowing that everything is taken care of.

5. Support and assistance If any issues or emergencies arise during your trip, a local travel agency or tour operator can provide support and assistance. They can help you navigate any

language barriers or cultural differences, and can provide assistance with medical emergencies, lost luggage, and other issues.

When choosing a local travel agency or tour operator, it is important to do your research and choose a reputable and reliable company. Look for companies that have good reviews and ratings, and that are registered and licensed with the appropriate authorities. It is also a good idea to compare prices and services to find the best option for your needs and budget.

In summary, using a local travel agency or tour operator can offer many benefits when planning a trip to Israel. They can provide local knowledge and expertise, tailored itineraries, cost savings, convenience and peace of mind, and support and assistance. Consider using a local travel agency or tour operator for your next trip to Israel for a more enjoyable and authentic travel experience

Maps and Transportation Schedules

When traveling to Israel, it is important to have access to maps and transportation schedules to help you navigate the country. Here are some resources and tips for finding maps and transportation schedules in Israel:

1. Tourist Information Centers Tourist information centers in Israel are a great resource for finding maps and transportation schedules. These centers are located throughout the country and offer a range of services, including free maps, transportation schedules, and information on local attractions and events.

2. Online Resources There are several online resources for finding maps and transportation schedules in Israel. The Israel Ministry of Tourism website offers a range of information on transportation options, including bus schedules, train schedules, and information on renting a car. Other

useful websites include the Israel Railways website and the Egged Bus website.

3. Mobile Apps There are several mobile apps that can help you navigate Israel, including maps and transportation schedules. The Moovit app is a popular choice, as it offers real-time information on bus and train schedules, as well as directions and maps. Other useful apps include Google Maps and Waze.

4. Local Transportation Offices If you are planning to use public transportation, you can also visit local transportation offices in Israel to find maps and schedules. These offices are located in most major cities and offer information on bus routes, train schedules, and other transportation options.

When using maps and transportation schedules in Israel, it is important to keep in mind that schedules and routes may be subject to change. It is always a good idea to double-check schedules and routes before you travel, particularly if you are planning to use public transportation. It is also important to be aware of any cultural or language barriers that may affect your ability to navigate the country.

There are several resources and tips for finding maps and transportation schedules in Israel. These include tourist information centers, online resources, mobile apps, and local transportation offices. By taking advantage of these resources, you can navigate Israel with ease and enjoy all that the country has to offer.

CHAPTER 3: ACCOMMODATIONS

Israel offers a range of accommodations to suit all budgets and travel styles. From luxury hotels to budget hostels, there are plenty of options to choose from. Here are some tips for finding the right accommodations in Israel:

1. Consider Your Budget Israel can be an expensive destination, particularly when it comes to accommodations. It is important to consider your budget when choosing accommodations. If you are on a tight budget, hostels and guesthouses are a good option. If you have a higher budget, there are plenty of luxury hotels and resorts to choose from.

2. Research Your Options There are many websites and resources available to help you research accommodations in Israel. Popular websites include Booking.com, Airbnb, and Hotels.com. You can also check out

travel guides and forums for recommendations from other travelers.

3. Check Location and Accessibility When choosing accommodations in Israel, it is important to consider the location and accessibility. If you are planning to do a lot of sightseeing, you may want to choose accommodations in a central location. If you are renting a car, you may want to choose accommodations with parking facilities. If you are relying on public transportation, you may want to choose accommodations close to a bus or train station.

4. Consider Your Travel Style Different types of accommodations suit different travel styles. If you are traveling solo or on a budget, hostels and guesthouses are a good option. If you are traveling with family or friends, you may want to consider renting an apartment or villa. If you

are looking for luxury and relaxation, there are plenty of resorts and hotels to choose from.

5. Book in Advance Israel can be a popular destination, particularly during peak season. It is important to book your accommodations in advance to ensure availability and avoid disappointment. This is particularly important if you are traveling during Jewish holidays or festivals.

There are many options for accommodations in Israel, including hostels, hotels, guesthouses, apartments, and resorts. It is important to consider your budget, location, accessibility, travel style, and book in advance when choosing accommodations. By taking the time to research your options, you can find the perfect accommodations to suit your needs and enjoy a comfortable and enjoyable stay in Israel.

Options for Hotels, Hostels, Guesthouses, and Rental Properties in Israel

Israel is a popular destination for tourists from all over the world due to its rich history, vibrant culture, and stunning natural landscapes. The country has a diverse range of accommodations to cater to different budgets and preferences, including hotels, hostels, guesthouses, and rental properties. In this Guide, we will explore the options available for visitors to Israel in each of these categories.

Hotels

Hotels are the most common type of accommodation for tourists in Israel, offering a range of amenities and services to make their stay comfortable and convenient. There are hotels of different categories and price ranges throughout the country, from luxury hotels in urban centers to more budget-friendly options in smaller towns and rural areas. Some of the most popular hotel chains in Israel include the Dan Hotels, Isrotel, and Fattal Hotels.

Luxury Hotels

For those looking for a more lavish experience, Israel has no shortage of high-end luxury hotels. These hotels offer world-class amenities, including fine dining restaurants, spas, fitness centers, and even private beaches. Some of the most popular luxury hotels in Israel include the King

David Hotel in Jerusalem, the Waldorf Astoria in Jerusalem, and the Ritz Carlton in Herzliya.

Business Hotels

Many hotels in Israel cater to business travelers, providing meeting rooms, conference facilities, and other amenities such as high-speed internet and business centers. Business hotels are often located in major cities and commercial centers such as Tel Aviv, Haifa, and Jerusalem. Popular options include the Sheraton Tel Aviv, Crowne Plaza Jerusalem, and Leonardo Hotel Haifa.

Boutique Hotels

Boutique hotels offer a more intimate and personalized experience, with unique designs and décor. These hotels often have fewer rooms than traditional hotels and are located in more secluded or niche areas such as the historic city of Safed or the desert oasis of Mitzpe Ramon. Popular boutique hotels in Israel include the Efendi Hotel in Akko, the Beresheet Hotel in Mitzpe Ramon, and the Villa Brown in Jerusalem.

Hostels

Hostels are a popular choice for budget-conscious travelers looking for affordable accommodation in Israel. Hostels offer a more social and communal experience, with shared dormitories, communal kitchens, and lounges. Many hostels also organize tours and activities for their guests, making them a great choice for solo travelers looking to meet new people. Some popular hostel chains in Israel include Abraham Hostels, Haifa Hostel, and Hayarkon 48 Hostel in Tel Aviv.

Budget-Friendly Hostels

Budget-friendly hostels offer a basic and affordable accommodation option for travelers on a tight budget. These hostels offer shared dormitories with bunk beds, communal bathrooms, and basic kitchen facilities. They are often located in urban centers and popular tourist destinations such as Jerusalem, Tel Aviv, and Eilat. Popular budget-friendly hostels in Israel include the Little Tel-Aviv Hostel, the Citadel Youth Hostel in Jerusalem, and the Haifa Bay View Hotel.

Luxury Hostels

Luxury hostels offer a more upscale and refined hostel experience, with private rooms, en-suite bathrooms, and high-end amenities such as rooftop terraces and swimming pools. These hostels are a great option for travelers who want to experience the social and communal atmosphere of a hostel while also enjoying some luxury and privacy. Popular luxury hostels in Israel include the Abraham Hostel in Tel Aviv, the Fauzi Azar Inn in Nazareth, and the Brown Beach House in Tel Aviv.

Guesthouses

Guesthouses are a type of accommodation that offers a more intimate and homely experience than traditional hotels. Guesthouses are often run by families or individuals who rent out rooms in their homes or properties. They offer a more personalized experience, with home-cooked meals, local recommendations, and a chance to interact with the local community. Guesthouses can be found in both urban and rural areas of Israel, and they are a great option for travelers who want to experience local culture and hospitality.

Rural Guesthouses

Rural guesthouses can be found in Israel's countryside, offering a peaceful retreat away from the hustle and bustle of the city. These guesthouses are often located in rural villages or on farms, offering guests the opportunity to experience rural life and agriculture. Many rural guesthouses offer activities such as hiking, horseback riding, and farm tours. Popular rural guesthouses in Israel include the Kibbutz Gonen Holiday Village in the Galilee region and the Neot Smadar Art Eco Village in the Negev Desert.

Urban Guesthouses

Urban guesthouses are located in urban centers such as Tel Aviv and Jerusalem, offering a more intimate and personalized experience than traditional hotels. Urban guesthouses are often located in historic buildings or neighborhoods, offering guests the opportunity to experience local culture and architecture. Popular urban guesthouses in Israel include the Villa Brown in Jerusalem, the Fabric Hotel in Tel Aviv, and the Little House in Bakah in Jerusalem.

Rental Properties

Rental properties are a popular choice for travelers who want to stay in a private and self-contained space, often with access to a kitchen and other amenities. Rental properties in Israel include apartments, villas, and vacation homes, and they can be found in both urban and rural areas of the country.

Vacation Rentals

Vacation rentals offer a private and self-contained space for travelers, often with access to a kitchen and other amenities such as a pool or garden. Vacation rentals are a popular choice for families and groups of friends who want to stay together in one place. They can be found in both urban and rural areas of Israel, and they offer a more flexible and customizable experience than traditional hotels. Popular vacation rentals in Israel include the Villa Marnin in Netanya, the Jerusalem Garden Apartment in Jerusalem, and the Villa Keren in Eilat.

Apartment Rentals

Apartment rentals are a popular choice for travelers who want to stay in urban centers such as Tel Aviv and Jerusalem. Apartment rentals offer a private and self-contained space, often with access to a kitchen and other amenities. They are a great option for travelers who want to experience local culture and nightlife while also having a comfortable and private space to relax. Popular apartment rentals in Israel include the Lev Tel Aviv Apartments in Tel Aviv, the Pomegranate Suite in Jerusalem, and the Jaffa Penthouse in Tel Aviv.

Villa Rentals

Villa rentals offer a more luxurious and private accommodation option for travelers, often with access to a pool, garden, and other high-end amenities. Villas can be found in both urban and rural areas of Israel, and they are a great option for families and groups of friends who want to stay together in a private and comfortable space. Popular villa rentals in Israel include the Villa Carmel in Haifa, the Villa Ronny in Netanya, and the Villa Van Gogh in Safed.

Israel offers a wide range of accommodations for travelers of all budgets and preferences. Whether you're looking for a luxury hotel in the heart of Tel Aviv, a budget-friendly hostel in Jerusalem, or a rural guesthouse in the Galilee region, there are plenty of options to choose from. By considering your budget, travel style, and preferred amenities, you can find the perfect accommodation to make your trip to Israel a memorable and enjoyable experience.

Recommendations for Budget, Mid-Range, And Luxury Accommodations In Different Parts Of The Country

Israel is a country with a diverse range of tourist attractions and accommodations, from bustling cities to tranquil beaches, and ancient historical sites to modern urban centers. No matter what your budget is, there are plenty of options for accommodation in Israel to suit all types of travelers. In this Guide, we will provide recommendations for budget, mid-range, and luxury accommodations in different parts of the country.

Budget Accommodations

For budget-conscious travelers, hostels and guesthouses are the most affordable options for accommodation in Israel. Hostels are a great way to save money on accommodation and meet other travelers from around the world.

Jerusalem

In Jerusalem, the Abraham Hostel is a popular choice for budget-conscious travelers. The hostel is located in the city center, within walking distance of many of Jerusalem's main attractions, including the Old City and the Machane Yehuda Market. The hostel offers a variety of room types, including dormitories and private rooms, as well as a communal kitchen, rooftop terrace, and daily tours and activities.

Tel Aviv

In Tel Aviv, the Florentin House is a popular hostel for budget-conscious travelers. The hostel is located in the trendy Florentin neighborhood, within walking distance of many of Tel Aviv's best restaurants, bars, and nightclubs. The hostel offers dormitories and private rooms, as well as a communal kitchen, rooftop terrace, and daily events and activities.

Haifa

In Haifa, the Port Inn is a popular hostel for budget-conscious travelers. The hostel is located in the heart of Haifa's German Colony, within walking distance of many of Haifa's main attractions, including the Bahai Gardens and the Haifa Port. The hostel offers dormitories and private rooms, as well as a communal kitchen and outdoor terrace.

Mid-Range Accommodations

For travelers who are looking for more comfort and amenities, mid-range accommodations such as hotels and guesthouses are a great option. These accommodations offer a balance between affordability and luxury, making them a great choice for many travelers.

Dead Sea

In the Dead Sea region, the Ein Gedi Hotel is a popular mid-range option for travelers. The hotel is located in the Ein Gedi Nature Reserve, surrounded by stunning desert landscapes and just a short distance from the Dead Sea. The hotel offers a variety of room types, including standard and deluxe rooms, as well as a spa, outdoor pool, and restaurant.

Galilee

In the Galilee region, the Ruth Rimonim Hotel is a popular mid-range option for travelers. The hotel is located in the town of Safed, within walking distance of many of Safed's main attractions, including the Old City and the artists' colony. The hotel offers a variety of room types, including standard and deluxe rooms, as well as a spa, indoor pool, and restaurant.

Eilat

In Eilat, the Dan Eilat Hotel is a popular mid-range option for travelers. The hotel is located on the beachfront, with stunning views of the Red Sea, and is within walking distance of many of Eilat's main attractions, including the Dolphin Reef and the Underwater Observatory. The hotel offers a variety of room types, including standard and deluxe rooms, as well as a spa, outdoor pool, and restaurant.

Luxury Accommodations

For travelers who are looking for a luxurious and indulgent experience, there are plenty of options for high-end accommodations in Israel. These accommodations offer top-of-the-line amenities and services, as well as stunning views and luxurious interiors.

Jerusalem

In Jerusalem, the Waldorf Astoria Jerusalem is a popular choice for luxury travelers. The hotel is located in a historic building in the heart of Jerusalem, with stunning views of the Old City and the Temple Mount. The hotel offers a variety of room types , including suites and deluxe rooms, as well as a spa, indoor pool, and fine dining restaurant.

Tel Aviv

In Tel Aviv, the Carlton Tel Aviv Hotel is a popular choice for luxury travelers. The hotel is located on the beachfront, with stunning views of the Mediterranean Sea, and is within walking distance of many of Tel Aviv's main attractions, including the Carmel Market and the Old Jaffa Port. The hotel offers a variety of room types, including suites and deluxe rooms, as well as a spa, outdoor pool, and fine dining restaurant.

Galilee

In the Galilee region, the Mizpe Hayamim Hotel is a popular choice for luxury travelers. The hotel is located on a hilltop, surrounded by lush greenery and stunning views of the Sea of Galilee. The hotel offers a variety of room types, including suites and deluxe rooms, as well as a spa, outdoor pool, and fine dining restaurant.

Eilat

In Eilat, the Herods Palace Hotel is a popular choice for luxury travelers. The hotel is located on the beachfront, with stunning views of the Red Sea, and is within walking distance of many of Eilat's main attractions, including the Dolphin Reef and the Underwater Observatory. The hotel offers a variety of room types, including suites and deluxe rooms, as well as a spa, outdoor pool, and fine dining restaurant.

Israel offers a wide range of accommodations to suit all types of travelers and budgets. From budget-friendly hostels and guesthouses to mid-range hotels and luxury resorts, there is something for everyone. When choosing your accommodation in Israel, consider your budget, location, and the amenities and services that are most important to you. With a little research and planning, you can find the perfect accommodation to make your trip to Israel unforgettable.

Information On Amenities and Services Offered by Each Type of Accommodation

When it comes to choosing the right type of accommodation for your trip to Israel, it's important to consider the amenities and services that are offered. Each type of accommodation, whether it's a budget hostel or a luxury hotel, has its own unique set of amenities and services. In this Guide, we will take a closer look at the amenities and services offered by each type of accommodation in Israel.

Budget Accommodations

Budget accommodations in Israel include hostels and guesthouses. These types of accommodations are ideal for travelers who are looking for affordable options that are still comfortable and clean. Here are some of the amenities and services that you can expect from budget accommodations in Israel:

1. Shared dormitory rooms or private rooms - Depending on the hostel or guesthouse, you may have the option of staying in a shared dormitory room with other travelers or a private room for a higher price.
2. Shared bathrooms - In most budget accommodations, you will share bathrooms with other guests.
3. Free Wi-Fi - Most budget accommodations offer free Wi-Fi to their guests.
4. Common areas - Budget accommodations typically have common areas where guests can relax and socialize with other travelers.
5. Kitchen facilities - Some hostels and guesthouses have kitchen facilities

where guests can prepare their own meals.

6. Laundry facilities - Some budget accommodations have laundry facilities for guests to use.

7. Tours and activities - Some hostels and guesthouses offer tours and activities for guests to participate in.

Mid-Range Accommodations

Mid-range accommodations in Israel include hotels and vacation rentals. These types of accommodations are ideal for travelers who are looking for comfortable and convenient options that are still affordable. Here are some of the amenities and services that you can expect from mid-range accommodations in Israel:

1. Private rooms with en suite bathrooms - Mid-range hotels and vacation rentals typically offer private rooms with en suite bathrooms.

2. Free Wi-Fi - Most mid-range accommodations offer free Wi-Fi to their guests.
3. On-site restaurants - Many mid-range hotels have on-site restaurants that serve breakfast, lunch, and dinner.
4. Fitness centers - Some mid-range hotels have fitness centers that guests can use.
5. Swimming pools - Some mid-range hotels and vacation rentals have swimming pools for guests to enjoy.
6. Business centers - Some mid-range hotels have business centers that guests can use to stay connected while on the road.
7. Concierge services - Many mid-range hotels offer concierge services to help guests with their travel needs.

Luxury Accommodations

Luxury accommodations in Israel include resorts and high-end hotels. These types of accommodations are ideal for travelers who are looking for luxury and pampering. Here are some of the amenities and services that you can expect from luxury accommodations in Israel:

1. Spacious suites with private balconies - Luxury hotels and resorts typically offer spacious suites with private balconies and stunning views.
2. Fine dining restaurants - Many luxury accommodations have on-site restaurants that offer gourmet dining experiences.
3. Spas and wellness centers - Luxury accommodations often have spas and wellness centers where guests can indulge in treatments and massages.
4. Fitness centers and yoga classes - Many luxury hotels and resorts have fitness centers and yoga classes for guests to stay active during their stay.
5. Swimming pools - Luxury hotels and resorts often have swimming pools that offer stunning views and are surrounded by beautiful gardens.

6. Beach access - Many luxury accommodations are located on the beachfront, offering guests direct access to the sea.
7. 24-hour room service and concierge services - Luxury hotels offer 24-hour room service and concierge services to ensure that guests have everything they need during their stay.

When choosing the right type of accommodation for your trip to Israel, it's important to consider the amenities and services that are offered. Budget accommodations are ideal for travelers who are looking for affordable options that still offer basic amenities such as free Wi-Fi, shared bathrooms, and common areas. Mid-range accommodations are perfect for those who want a comfortable and convenient stay with added amenities such as on-site restaurants, fitness centers, and swimming pools. Luxury accommodations, on the other hand, offer a high-end experience with amenities such as spacious suites, fine dining restaurants, spas and wellness centers, and 24-hour room service and concierge services.

Ultimately, the type of accommodation you choose depends on your budget, travel style, and personal preferences. Whether you opt for a budget hostel or a luxury resort, there are plenty of options available throughout Israel that cater to different travelers' needs.

Tips for Booking and Navigating Accommodations in Israel

Israel is a popular destination for travelers from all over the world, and finding the right accommodation can be a challenge. With so many options available, it's important to do your research and follow some tips to ensure that you find the perfect place to stay during your visit. In this Guide, we'll share some tips for booking and navigating accommodations in Israel.

1. Determine your budget

Before you start looking for accommodations in Israel, it's important to determine your budget. Israel has a wide range of accommodations, from budget hostels to luxury resorts, so knowing how much you can afford to spend will help you narrow down your options.

2. Consider your travel style

Another factor to consider when choosing accommodations in Israel is your travel style. Are you traveling alone or with a group? Are you looking for a social experience or a more private one? Do you prefer to stay in the city center or in a quieter location? Answering these questions will help you choose the right type of accommodation that fits your travel style.

3. Research the area

Israel is a diverse country with many different regions and cities to explore. Before booking accommodations, it's important to research the area where you plan to stay. Look at the neighborhood, the distance from popular attractions, and the safety of the area. This will help you choose the right location for your stay.

4. Read reviews

One of the best ways to gauge the quality of accommodations in Israel is to read reviews from other travelers. Websites like TripAdvisor and Booking.com offer a wealth of information from real people who have stayed in the same accommodations you're considering. Look for reviews that mention the cleanliness of the rooms, the friendliness of the staff, and the overall experience of the stay.

5. Book in advance

Israel is a popular destination, particularly during peak travel seasons, so it's important to book your accommodations in advance to ensure availability. This is especially true if you're looking to stay in a popular area or during a major holiday or event.

6. Consider alternative accommodations

In addition to hotels, there are other types of accommodations available in Israel that may be worth considering. Hostels, guesthouses, vacation rentals, and bed and breakfasts are all options that can offer a unique and affordable experience. Researching and considering these alternative accommodations can help you find a place to stay that fits your budget and travel style.

7. Check for amenities

Before booking accommodations in Israel, make sure to check for amenities such as

Wi-Fi, air conditioning, and breakfast. Some accommodations may offer additional amenities like swimming pools, gyms, and on-site restaurants, so make sure to check what is included with your stay.

8. Communicate your needs

If you have specific needs or requests, such as a room on a higher floor or a gluten-free breakfast, it's important to communicate these to the accommodations before booking. Many places will do their best to accommodate your needs, but they need to know what they are in advance.

9. Understand the check-in and check-out process

Make sure you understand the check-in and check-out process for your accommodations in Israel. Some places may require a deposit or payment in advance, while others may have specific check-in times. Understanding the process ahead of time can help avoid any confusion or issues during your stay.

10. Plan your transportation

Finally, when booking accommodations in Israel, it's important to consider transportation. If you're staying in a remote location, you may need to rent a car or take public transportation to get around. Alternatively, if you're staying in a city center, you may be able to walk to many of the popular attractions. Understanding transportation options and planning accordingly can help make your stay in Israel more enjoyable.

Booking and navigating accommodations in Israel can be a challenge, but by following these tips, you can find the perfect place to stay during your visit. Remember to determine your budget, consider your travel style, research the area, read reviews, book in advance, consider alternative accommodations, check for amenities, communicate your needs, understand the check-in and check-out process, and plan your transportation. By doing so, you can have a comfortable and enjoyable stay in Israel.

Top Hotels in Israel

Israel is home to many world-class hotels that offer luxurious accommodations and exceptional service to travelers from all over the world. From the bustling city of Tel Aviv to the tranquil beaches of Eilat, there are a wide variety of hotels to choose from, each with its unique style and amenities. In this Guide, we'll highlight some of the top hotels in Israel.

1. The King David Hotel, Jerusalem

The King David Hotel is one of the most iconic and prestigious hotels in Israel. Located in the heart of Jerusalem, this historic hotel has been welcoming guests since 1931 and has played host to countless dignitaries, celebrities, and world leaders. The hotel features 233 elegant rooms and suites, a fitness center, swimming pool, spa, and several on-site dining options.

The King David Hotel also boasts stunning views of the Old City of Jerusalem and is just a short walk from many of the city's most famous attractions.

2. The Waldorf Astoria Jerusalem

The Waldorf Astoria Jerusalem is a luxurious and elegant hotel located in the heart of the city's historic center. The hotel occupies a beautifully restored 1920s building and features 226 rooms and suites, each decorated with a combination of contemporary and classic design elements.

The Waldorf Astoria Jerusalem also boasts several dining options, a spa, and a rooftop terrace with panoramic views of the city.

3. The Norman Tel Aviv

The Norman Tel Aviv is a boutique hotel located in the heart of the city's bustling center. The hotel features 50 stylishly decorated rooms and suites, each with its unique character and design. The Norman Tel Aviv also boasts several on-site dining options, including a rooftop restaurant and bar, a swimming pool, and a spa. The hotel's central location makes it an ideal base for exploring the city's many attractions, including the beach, museums, and nightlife.

4. The Ritz-Carlton Herzliya

The Ritz-Carlton Herzliya is a luxurious seaside hotel located just north of Tel Aviv. The hotel features 115 elegant rooms and suites, each with its balcony offering stunning views of the Mediterranean Sea. The Ritz-Carlton Herzliya also boasts several dining options, a spa, and a rooftop infinity pool. The hotel's location makes it an ideal base for exploring the nearby marina, beaches, and the vibrant city of Tel Aviv.

5. The Beresheet Hotel, Mitzpe Ramon

The Beresheet Hotel is a luxury desert retreat located in the heart of the Negev Desert. The hotel features 111 rooms and suites, each with its private balcony offering breathtaking views of the surrounding landscape. The Beresheet Hotel also boasts several on-site dining options, a spa, and a swimming pool. The hotel's location makes it an ideal base for exploring the nearby Ramon Crater and other natural attractions in the Negev Desert.

6. The Setai Tel Aviv

The Setai Tel Aviv is a luxurious beachfront hotel located in the heart of the city's vibrant center. The hotel features 120 stylishly decorated rooms and suites, each with its balcony offering stunning views of the Mediterranean Sea. The Setai Tel Aviv also boasts several on-site dining options, a spa, and a rooftop infinity pool. The hotel's central location makes it an ideal base for exploring the city's many attractions, including the beach, museums, and nightlife.

7. The Dan Tel Aviv Hotel

The Dan Tel Aviv Hotel is a luxurious beachfront hotel located in the heart of the city's vibrant center. The hotel features 280 elegant rooms and suites, each decorated in a modern and stylish design. The Dan Tel Aviv Hotel also boasts several on-site dining options, a swimming pool, and a spa. The hotel's central location makes it an ideal base for exploring the city's many attractions, including the beach, museums, and nightlife.

8. The Carlton Tel Aviv

The Carlton Tel Aviv is a luxurious beachfront hotel located in the heart of Tel Aviv's vibrant center. The hotel features 270 elegant rooms and suites, each decorated in a modern and stylish design. The Carlton Tel Aviv also boasts several on-site dining options, a swimming pool, and a spa. The hotel's location makes it an ideal base for exploring the nearby beaches, shops, and restaurants.

9. The Mamilla Hotel, Jerusalem

The Mamilla Hotel is a luxurious and modern hotel located just a short walk from the Old City of Jerusalem. The hotel features 194 elegantly decorated rooms and suites, each with its balcony offering stunning views of the city. The Mamilla Hotel also boasts several on-site dining options, a spa, and a rooftop terrace with panoramic views of Jerusalem. The hotel's central location makes it an ideal base for exploring the city's many attractions, including the Western Wall and the Church of the Holy Sepulchre.

10. The David InterContinental Tel Aviv

The David InterContinental Tel Aviv is a luxurious beachfront hotel located in the heart of the city's vibrant center. The hotel features 555 elegant rooms and suites, each with its balcony offering stunning views of the Mediterranean Sea. The David InterContinental Tel Aviv also boasts several on-site dining options, a swimming pool, and a spa. The hotel's central location makes it an ideal base for exploring the nearby beaches, shops, and restaurants.

Israel is home to many world-class hotels that offer luxurious accommodations, exceptional service, and stunning views to travelers from all over the world. Whether you're looking for a beachfront getaway in Tel Aviv or a luxurious desert retreat in the Negev, there are many options to choose from. By researching the area, determining your budget, and considering your travel style, you can find the perfect hotel to suit your needs and make your stay in Israel unforgettable.

CHAPTER 4: FOOD AND DRINK

Food and drink are an important aspect of Israeli culture, with a rich culinary history that reflects the country's diverse population and cultural influences. From traditional Middle Eastern dishes to international cuisine, Israeli food and drink offer a unique and delicious experience for visitors to the country.

Israeli Cuisine

Israeli cuisine is characterized by its fusion of Jewish, Arabic, and

Mediterranean culinary traditions. The country's cuisine is heavily influenced by the Middle East, with popular dishes including hummus, falafel, and shakshuka. Other popular dishes include sabich (an Iraqi sandwich filled with eggplant and hard-boiled eggs), schnitzel (breaded and fried chicken or beef cutlets), and burekas (flaky pastries filled with cheese, potato, or meat).

Israeli cuisine also incorporates many fresh vegetables and herbs, such as tomatoes, cucumbers, parsley, and mint. Olive oil, lemon juice, and garlic are commonly used to season dishes, and spices like cumin, coriander, and turmeric are frequently used in Middle Eastern cooking.

In addition to traditional Israeli cuisine, the country's food scene has also been influenced by international cuisine, with many trendy restaurants serving up fusion dishes that blend Israeli flavors with European, Asian, and African influences.

Israeli Drinks

Israel is home to a burgeoning wine industry, with several world-renowned wineries located throughout the country. The region's Mediterranean climate and diverse terroir make it an ideal location for growing a wide variety of grape varietals, and Israeli wines have won numerous awards and accolades in recent years.

In addition to wine, Israel is also known for its beer, with several craft breweries producing high-quality brews that are popular with locals and tourists alike. Some of the most popular Israeli beers include Goldstar, Maccabee, and Taybeh.

Israel is also a major producer of arak, a traditional Middle Eastern liquor made from anise and distilled grapes. Arak is often served with water and ice, and is a popular drink in restaurants and bars throughout the country.

Traditional Israeli Beverages

One of the most popular traditional Israeli beverages is tea, which is often served with fresh mint or other herbs. Another popular drink is coffee, with many trendy cafes throughout the country serving up high-quality espresso and specialty drinks.

In addition to tea and coffee, Israel is also known for its fresh fruit juices, with vendors selling everything from freshly squeezed orange juice to exotic juices made from pomegranate, grapefruit, and passionfruit.

Kosher Food in Israel

Kosher food is an important aspect of Jewish dietary laws, and many restaurants and cafes throughout Israel offer kosher options. Kosher food is prepared according to strict dietary guidelines, which prohibit the consumption of certain animals (such as pigs and shellfish) and require the separation of meat and dairy products.

Many kosher restaurants in Israel offer a wide variety of traditional Jewish dishes, such as matzo ball soup, brisket, and kugel. In addition to traditional Jewish cuisine, many kosher restaurants also offer international cuisine that has been adapted to meet kosher dietary laws.

Street Food in Israel

Israel is also known for its vibrant street food scene, with vendors selling everything from falafel and shawarma to hummus and sabich. One of the most popular street foods in Israel is falafel, which is made from ground chickpeas and served in a pita with hummus, tahini, and fresh vegetables.

Shawarma, which is made from slow-roasted meat that is thinly sliced and served in a pita with vegetables and sauce, is also a popular street food in Israel. Other popular street foods include bourekas (flaky pastries filled with cheese, potato, or meat), malawach (a Yemenite pastry filled with cheese or other toppings), and knafeh (a sweet dessert made with shredded phyllo dough, cheese, and syrup).

Vegetarian and Vegan Options

Israel is also a great destination for vegetarian and vegan travelers, with many restaurants and cafes offering a wide variety of plant-based options. In addition to traditional Israeli dishes like hummus and falafel (which are naturally vegan), many restaurants also offer vegetarian and vegan versions of traditional Jewish dishes like matzo ball soup and latkes.

Many trendy cafes and restaurants throughout the country also offer innovative vegetarian and vegan dishes that blend Israeli flavors with international influences. For example, you might find a vegan shakshuka made with tofu instead of eggs, or a vegetarian sabich filled with grilled vegetables instead of eggplant.

Food and Drink Festivals

Israel is home to several food and drink festivals throughout the year, which showcase the country's rich culinary traditions and diverse food scene. Some of the most popular food and drink festivals in Israel include:

- Tel Aviv Eat - A four-day food festival held in Tel Aviv that showcases the city's vibrant food scene, with vendors serving up a wide variety of international and Israeli cuisine.

- Jerusalem Wine Festival - A two-day festival held in the gardens of the Israel Museum, where visitors can sample wines from over 50 different wineries.
- Taste of Israel - A three-day festival held in Eilat that celebrates Israeli food and drink, with vendors serving up everything from street food to gourmet dishes.
- Beer Festival - A two-day festival held in Tel Aviv that showcases Israel's burgeoning craft beer scene, with breweries from throughout the country offering tastings and events.

In addition to these festivals, many cities and towns throughout Israel also host food and drink events throughout the year, such as wine tastings, culinary tours, and cooking workshops.

Israeli food and drink offer a unique and delicious experience for visitors to the country, with a rich culinary history that reflects the country's diverse population and cultural influences. Whether you're a meat lover, vegetarian, or vegan, there are plenty of options to suit all tastes and dietary preferences. So be sure to explore the country's vibrant food scene and indulge in some of the delicious dishes and drinks that Israel has to offer!

Overview of Israeli Cuisine and Regional Specialties

Israeli cuisine is a diverse and flavorful fusion of Jewish, Mediterranean, Middle Eastern, and North African influences. The country's location at the crossroads of Asia, Europe, and Africa, as well as its history of immigration and cultural exchange, has resulted in a unique culinary heritage that is both traditional and modern.

Regional Specialties

Israel's diverse landscape and climate has also influenced its regional cuisine, with each region offering its own unique dishes and ingredients. Some of the most popular regional specialties include:

1. Jerusalem: Located in the Judean Hills, Jerusalem is known for its hearty, slow-cooked stews and meat

dishes, such as lamb shawarma and kubbeh soup (made with bulgur wheat and meat). The city is also famous for its street food, including falafel, hummus, and shakshuka.

2. Tel Aviv: As Israel's cosmopolitan hub, Tel Aviv is a melting pot of culinary influences from around the world. The city's cuisine is characterized by its fresh, seasonal ingredients and modern twists on traditional dishes, such as sabich (an Iraqi sandwich made with grilled eggplant, hard-boiled eggs, and tahini) and burekas (savory pastries filled with cheese or meat).

3. Haifa: Located on the northern coast of Israel, Haifa is known for its fresh seafood, such as grilled sea bream and shrimp kebabs. The city is also home to the popular street food dish, falafel with fries, which is served in pita bread with salad and tahini.

4. Galilee: The Galilee region is known for its rustic, home-style cooking, with an emphasis on locally sourced ingredients and slow-cooked stews. Some popular dishes include stuffed grape leaves, maqluba (an Arabic rice and meat dish), and labneh (a creamy yogurt cheese).

5. Negev: The desert region of the Negev is known for its Bedouin cuisine, which is based on a nomadic lifestyle and the use of simple ingredients. Popular dishes include lamb and chicken cooked in a pit, and Bedouin tea (made with sage and mint).

Traditional Israeli Dishes

In addition to regional specialties, Israeli cuisine is also characterized by a few staple dishes that are enjoyed throughout the country:

1. Hummus: A creamy dip made from chickpeas, tahini, lemon juice, and garlic. It is typically served with pita bread, vegetables, and olives.
2. Falafel: Deep-fried balls or patties made from ground chickpeas, herbs, and spices. They are typically served in pita bread with salad, tahini, and pickles.
3. Shakshuka: A breakfast dish made from eggs poached in a tomato and pepper sauce, seasoned with cumin, paprika, and chili flakes.
4. Sabich: A popular street food sandwich made with grilled eggplant, hard-boiled eggs, hummus, tahini, and salad.
5. Shawarma: Thinly sliced meat (usually chicken or lamb) cooked on a rotating spit and served in a pita bread with salad, hummus, and tahini.
6. Borekas: Savory pastries filled with cheese, potato, or meat, and typically served as a snack or breakfast food.

7. Kibbeh: A Levantine dish made from ground meat and bulgur wheat, seasoned with spices and herbs. It is typically served fried or baked.

Israeli cuisine offers a rich and flavorful culinary experience, with a fusion of Jewish, Mediterranean, Middle Eastern, and North African influences. Whether you're exploring regional specialties or enjoying traditional Israeli dishes, there is something to suit every palate. So be sure to indulge in some of the country's culinary delights during your visit to Israel.

Recommendations for Must-Try Dishes and Local Restaurants

Israel is a melting pot of cultures and cuisines, making it a food lover's paradise. From traditional Middle Eastern dishes to modern twists on classic Israeli fare, there is no shortage of delicious food to try. Here are some must-try dishes and local restaurants to check out during your visit to Israel:

Must-Try Dishes

1. Hummus - Hummus is a staple in Israeli cuisine, and there are many different variations to try. Some popular toppings include chickpeas, tahini, paprika, and olive oil. Be sure to pair it with fresh pita bread for the ultimate experience.
2. Shakshuka - Shakshuka is a popular breakfast dish made with eggs poached in a spicy tomato sauce. It's usually served with crusty bread or pita for dipping.
3. Falafel - Falafel is a popular street food in Israel made from ground chickpeas, spices, and herbs. It's usually served in a pita with salad and tahini sauce.
4. Sabich - Sabich is a popular Israeli sandwich made with fried eggplant, hard-boiled eggs, hummus, tahini, and

Israeli salad (tomatoes, cucumbers, and onions).

5. Shawarma - Shawarma is a Middle Eastern sandwich made with roasted meat (usually chicken or lamb), salad, and tahini sauce. It's usually served in a pita or laffa bread.

6. Burekas - Burekas are savory pastries filled with cheese, potato, or meat. They're perfect for a quick snack or breakfast on the go.

7. Malabi - Malabi is a sweet pudding made with milk, cornstarch, and rosewater. It's usually topped with crushed nuts, coconut, or syrup.

Local Restaurants

1. Abu Hassan - Abu Hassan is a legendary hummus restaurant in Jaffa that has been serving up some of the best hummus in Israel for over 50 years. It's a small, no-frills place with

a limited menu, but the hummus is worth the trip alone.

2. Carmel Market - The Carmel Market in Tel Aviv is a bustling market filled with vendors selling fresh produce, spices, and street food. It's the perfect place to sample Israeli cuisine and get a taste of local life.

3. HaSalon - HaSalon is a trendy restaurant in Tel Aviv that serves modern Israeli cuisine with a twist. The menu changes regularly, but some popular dishes include the beef tartare and roasted cauliflower.

4. Machneyuda - Machneyuda is a lively restaurant in Jerusalem that's known for its creative Israeli cuisine and lively atmosphere. The menu is based on seasonal and local ingredients, and the dishes are designed for sharing.

5. M25 - M25 is a hidden gem in Haifa that serves up traditional Middle Eastern dishes in a cozy, intimate

setting. Be sure to try the stuffed grape leaves and the lamb kebabs.

6. Tishbi - Tishbi is a family-owned winery and restaurant in the heart of the Galilee region. They serve a variety of Israeli dishes, including cheese platters, grilled meats, and fresh salads. And of course, the wine is excellent.

7. Uri Buri - Uri Buri is a seafood restaurant in Acre that's considered one of the best in Israel. The menu changes daily based on the freshest catch of the day, but some popular dishes include the crab cakes and the sea bream.

Israel's diverse culinary scene offers something for every palate. Whether you're looking for traditional Middle Eastern dishes or modern twists on classic Israeli fare, there are plenty of must-try dishes and local restaurants to explore during your visit. So be sure to come hungry and ready to indulge in the delicious food and drink scene in Israel.

Dietary Restrictions and Considerations for Travelers

When traveling to a new destination, it's important to consider any dietary restrictions or preferences you may have. Israel is a diverse country with a wide range of culinary offerings, but it's also important to be mindful of dietary considerations, such as food allergies, religious dietary restrictions, and vegan or vegetarian preferences. Here are some tips and considerations for travelers with dietary restrictions:

Food Allergies

If you have food allergies, it's important to be vigilant when dining out in Israel. While most restaurants are aware of common allergens like nuts, shellfish, and gluten, it's still a good idea to inform your server about your specific allergies. If you're not confident in your ability to communicate your allergy in Hebrew, it may be helpful to carry a translated card or app that outlines your allergies in the local language.

Religious Dietary Restrictions

Israel is a deeply religious country, and both Jewish and Muslim dietary restrictions are widely observed. Jewish dietary laws, known as kashrut, prohibit the consumption of certain foods, such as pork and shellfish, and require that meat and dairy products be kept separate. Similarly, Islamic dietary laws, known as halal, prohibit the consumption of pork and require that meat be prepared in a specific way.

If you follow these dietary laws, it's important to seek out restaurants that cater to your needs. Many restaurants in Israel have kashrut or halal certifications, and you can also find kosher or halal food stands in markets and street food vendors. It's also important to be aware that not all Jewish or

Muslim restaurants follow the same strict guidelines, so it's always a good idea to ask about the specific preparations and ingredients used.

Vegan and Vegetarian Diets

Veganism and vegetarianism are growing trends in Israel, and there are plenty of options for travelers who follow these diets. Many restaurants and cafes in Tel Aviv, in particular, cater to vegans and vegetarians, with plant-based menus and dairy-free options.

If you're following a vegan or vegetarian diet, it's still a good idea to check with your server about any hidden animal products or dairy that may be used in dishes. Additionally, if you're traveling to more rural or remote areas, it may be more difficult to find vegan or vegetarian options, so it's always a good idea to plan ahead and bring snacks or meal options.

Other Considerations

In addition to the above considerations, it's also important to be mindful of food safety and hygiene when dining out in Israel. While the country generally has high standards of cleanliness and food safety, it's still a good idea to avoid street food vendors that may not adhere to the same standards. Additionally, be sure to drink bottled or filtered water, and avoid tap water and ice in drinks.

Whether you have specific dietary restrictions or simply prefer certain types of cuisine, there are plenty of options for food and drink in Israel. By being mindful of your dietary needs and preferences, you can enjoy all the delicious culinary offerings that the country has to offer while staying healthy and safe on your travels.

CHAPTER 5: ACTIVITIES AND ATTRACTIONS

Israel is a small country that offers a wide variety of activities and attractions for travelers. From exploring historic and religious sites to enjoying the beautiful beaches and natural scenery, there is something for everyone in Israel. Here are some top activities and attractions to consider when planning your trip:

1. Visit the Old City of Jerusalem - Jerusalem is one of the world's most historic and religiously significant cities. The Old City is home to many religious sites, including the Western Wall, the Church of the Holy Sepulchre, and the Dome of the Rock. Visitors can wander through the narrow streets and marketplaces, learning about the city's history and significance.

2. Relax on the Beaches - Israel is home to many beautiful beaches, including

Tel Aviv's famous beaches. Visitors can soak up the sun, swim in the Mediterranean Sea, and enjoy water sports like surfing, paddleboarding, and kiteboarding.

3. Explore the Desert - Israel's desert landscape is rugged and beautiful, with opportunities for hiking, biking, and off-roading. The Negev Desert is home to stunning natural attractions like the Ramon Crater and the Ein Gedi Nature Reserve.

4. Visit the Dead Sea - The Dead Sea is one of the world's most unique natural wonders, known for its salty, mineral-rich waters that allow visitors to float effortlessly. The area also offers opportunities for spa treatments, hiking, and exploring nearby historic sites like Masada.

5. Tour Wineries and Vineyards - Israel's wine industry has been growing in recent years, with many boutique wineries and vineyards offering tours

and tastings. Visitors can sample a variety of wines made from indigenous grape varieties and learn about the history of winemaking in Israel.

6. Experience the Nightlife - Tel Aviv is known for its vibrant nightlife scene, with bars, clubs, and live music venues open late into the night. Visitors can enjoy a night out on the town, sampling local beers and cocktails, and listening to live music.

7. Visit Masada - Masada is an ancient fortress that sits atop a mountain overlooking the Dead Sea. The site is rich in history, with its famous siege by the Roman army in 73 AD. Visitors can take a cable car to the top of the mountain and explore the ruins of the fortress, learning about its significance in Jewish history.

8. Explore the Galilee - The Galilee region in northern Israel is known for its beautiful countryside, historic sites, and religious significance. Visitors can

explore the ancient city of Tiberias, visit historic sites like the Church of the Multiplication of Loaves and Fishes, and hike in the beautiful Mount Meron Nature Reserve.

9. Visit Tel Aviv's Museums - Tel Aviv is home to many world-class museums, including the Tel Aviv Museum of Art and the Museum of the Jewish People. Visitors can explore art, history, and culture in these fascinating institutions.

10. Go on a Food Tour - Israel's cuisine is a unique blend of Mediterranean, Middle Eastern, and Jewish flavors. Visitors can explore the country's food scene on a guided food tour, sampling local specialties like hummus, falafel, and shakshuka.

These are just a few of the many activities and attractions to enjoy in Israel. With so much to see and do, travelers are sure to have a memorable and exciting trip.

Popular Tourist Destinations

Israel is a country that has been attracting visitors for centuries due to its historical and religious significance, natural beauty, and vibrant culture. From the ancient city of Jerusalem to the modern metropolis of Tel Aviv, there are countless popular tourist destinations in Israel that are worth exploring. In this Guide, we will explore some of the most popular tourist destinations in Israel.

Jerusalem

Jerusalem is one of the oldest and most historically significant cities in the world. It is revered by Jews, Christians, and Muslims as a holy city, and it is home to some of the most important religious sites in the world. The Old City of Jerusalem is a UNESCO World Heritage Site, and it is divided into four quarters: the Jewish Quarter, the Christian Quarter, the Muslim Quarter, and the Armenian Quarter.

One of the most popular attractions in Jerusalem is the Western Wall, also known as the Wailing Wall. It is the last remaining part of the Second Temple, which was destroyed by the Romans in 70 CE. The Western Wall is a place of prayer and reflection for Jews, and visitors can leave notes with their prayers in the cracks of the wall.

Another must-see attraction in Jerusalem is the Church of the Holy Sepulchre, which is believed to be the site of Jesus' crucifixion and burial. The church is a complex of buildings, including the tomb of Jesus and the Chapel of the Finding of the Cross.

Other popular attractions in Jerusalem include the Mount of Olives, the Dome of the Rock, and the Yad Vashem Holocaust Memorial Museum.

Tel Aviv

Tel Aviv is the second-largest city in Israel, and it is known for its modern architecture, sandy beaches, and vibrant nightlife. The city was founded in 1909, and it has a unique mix of European and Middle Eastern influences.

One of the most popular tourist destinations in Tel Aviv is the beach. Tel Aviv has a 14-kilometer stretch of sandy beaches, which are popular with locals and tourists alike. The beaches are perfect for swimming, sunbathing, and surfing.

Another popular attraction in Tel Aviv is the White City, which is a collection of over 4,000 Bauhaus-style buildings that were built in the 1930s. The White City is a UNESCO World Heritage Site, and it is known for its clean lines and simple design.

Other popular attractions in Tel Aviv include the Carmel Market, the Nachalat Binyamin Crafts Fair, and the Tel Aviv Museum of Art.

Haifa

Haifa is the third-largest city in Israel, and it is known for its beautiful gardens, stunning views, and cultural diversity. The city is built on the slopes of Mount Carmel, and it offers panoramic views of the Mediterranean Sea.

One of the most popular attractions in Haifa is the Bahai Gardens. The gardens are a UNESCO World Heritage Site, and they are considered one of the most beautiful gardens in the world. The gardens consist of

19 terraces that are filled with colorful flowers and shrubs.

Another popular attraction in Haifa is the Stella Maris Monastery, which is located on the summit of Mount Carmel. The monastery is believed to have been built on the site where the prophet Elijah lived, and it offers stunning views of the city and the sea.

Other popular attractions in Haifa include the Haifa Zoo, the Haifa Museum of Art, and the German Colony.

Eilat

Eilat is a resort town located on the southern tip of Israel, on the shores of the Red Sea. It is known for its beautiful beaches, crystal-clear waters, and vibrant coral reefs. Eilat is a popular destination for snorkeling, diving, and other water sports.

One of the most popular attractions in Eilat is the Coral Beach Nature Reserve. The Coral Beach Nature Reserve is home to a vibrant coral reef that is teeming with marine life. Visitors can go snorkeling or scuba diving to explore the reef and see colorful fish, turtles, and other sea creatures.

Another popular attraction in Eilat is the Dolphin Reef, which is a unique ecological site where visitors can swim and interact with dolphins in their natural habitat. The Dolphin Reef also offers educational programs about marine conservation and the importance of protecting dolphins and other sea creatures.

Other popular attractions in Eilat include the Underwater Observatory Marine Park, which offers a glimpse into the Red Sea's underwater world through an underwater observation deck and aquariums, and the Timna Park, which is a stunning desert park that is home to ancient copper mines, rock formations, and hiking trails.

Dead Sea

The Dead Sea is a saltwater lake located on the border between Israel and Jordan. It is known for its high salt and mineral content, which is believed to have therapeutic properties for the skin and body. The Dead Sea is also the lowest point on earth, with its surface sitting more than 400 meters below sea level.

One of the most popular attractions in the Dead Sea is the Ein Gedi Nature Reserve, which is a stunning oasis that is home to waterfalls, streams, and a variety of plant and animal species. Visitors can go hiking in the reserve, take a dip in the natural pools, or enjoy a spa treatment using the mineral-rich mud and water from the Dead Sea.

Another popular attraction in the Dead Sea is Masada, which is an ancient fortress that sits on top of a steep hill overlooking the Dead Sea. Masada is a UNESCO World Heritage Site, and it is a symbol of Jewish resistance against the Romans.

Other popular activities in the Dead Sea area include floating in the salty water of the sea, visiting the Qumran Caves where the Dead Sea Scrolls were discovered, and taking a jeep tour through the surrounding desert landscape.

Nazareth

Nazareth is a city in northern Israel that is known for its rich Christian history and cultural significance. It is believed to be the childhood home of Jesus, and it is home to some of the most important Christian pilgrimage sites in the world.

One of the most popular attractions in Nazareth is the Basilica of the Annunciation, which is a stunning church that is built on the site where the angel Gabriel is believed to have appeared to Mary to announce that she would give birth to Jesus. The church is a pilgrimage site for Catholics and Orthodox Christians, and it houses beautiful artwork and mosaics.

Another popular attraction in Nazareth is the Nazareth Village, which is a living museum that recreates life in the Galilee region during the time of Jesus. Visitors can see demonstrations of traditional crafts and agriculture, and they can learn about the customs and traditions of the people who lived in the region 2,000 years ago.

Other popular attractions in Nazareth include the Church of St. Joseph, which is believed to be the site of Joseph's carpentry workshop, and the Old City Market, which is a bustling bazaar filled with spices, textiles, and handicrafts.

Israel is a country that offers a rich blend of history, religion, culture, and natural beauty. From the ancient city of Jerusalem to the modern metropolis of Tel Aviv, from the stunning beaches of Eilat to the therapeutic waters of the Dead Sea, and from the cultural diversity of Haifa to the Christian heritage of Nazareth, there are countless popular tourist destinations in Israel that are worth exploring. Whether you are a history buff, a nature lover, or a religious pilgrim, Israel has something to offer for everyone.

Outdoor Activities

Israel is a small country located in the Middle East, with a diverse landscape that offers a wide range of outdoor activities for visitors and locals alike. From hiking in the desert to swimming in the Mediterranean Sea, there is something for everyone to enjoy in Israel's great outdoors.

Hiking and Trekking

One of the most popular outdoor activities in Israel is hiking and trekking. The country has a vast network of hiking trails that offer stunning views of the desert, mountains, and coastline. Some of the most famous hiking trails in Israel include the Israel National Trail, the Jesus Trail, and the Masada Trail.

The Israel National Trail is a 1000-kilometer-long trail that runs from the northern border of Israel to the southernmost point of the country. It takes around 6-8 weeks to complete the entire trail, but many people choose to hike smaller sections of it. The trail passes through a variety of landscapes, including forests, mountains, and deserts, and offers breathtaking views of the Mediterranean Sea.

The Jesus Trail is a 65-kilometer-long trail that follows in the footsteps of Jesus, from Nazareth to the Sea of Galilee. The trail passes through historic sites, such as the Mount of Beatitudes and Capernaum, and offers stunning views of the Galilee region.

The Masada Trail is a challenging hike that leads to the top of Masada, an ancient fortress located in the Judean Desert. The trail is steep and requires a good level of fitness, but the views from the top are worth the effort.

Cycling

Cycling is another popular outdoor activity in Israel, with a growing number of dedicated cycling routes throughout the country. Some of the most popular cycling routes in Israel include the Israel Bike Trail, the Tel Aviv Promenade, and the Haifa to Akko route.

The Israel Bike Trail is a 1400-kilometer-long cycling route that runs from the northern border of Israel to the southernmost point of the country. It passes through a variety of landscapes, including forests, mountains, and deserts, and offers stunning views of the Mediterranean Sea.

The Tel Aviv Promenade is a 14-kilometer-long cycling route that runs along the coastline of Tel Aviv. It is a popular route for both locals and tourists, with stunning views of the Mediterranean Sea and the city skyline.

The Haifa to Akko route is a 25-kilometer-long cycling route that runs along the coastline between the cities of Haifa and Akko. It offers stunning views of the Mediterranean Sea and passes through historic sites, such as the Crusader Fortress in Akko.

Water Activities

Israel's location on the Mediterranean Sea and the Red Sea makes it an ideal destination for water activities. Some of the most popular water activities in Israel include swimming, snorkeling, scuba diving, and windsurfing.

The Mediterranean Sea offers warm and calm waters, making it an ideal spot for swimming and snorkeling. Some of the best beaches in Israel include Tel Aviv Beach, Herzliya Beach, and Bat Yam Beach.

The Red Sea is a popular destination for scuba diving and snorkeling, with crystal clear waters and a variety of marine life. The city of Eilat is a popular destination for water activities, with a range of diving schools and equipment rental shops.

Windsurfing is also a popular activity in Israel, with the city of Tel Aviv offering some of the best windsurfing conditions in the country. The city's strong winds and calm waters make it an ideal spot for beginners and experts alike.

Desert Activities

Israel's desert landscape offers a range of outdoor activities, including camel riding, jeep tours, and hot air balloon rides.

Camel riding is a popular activity in the Negev Desert, with tours available that offer stunning views of the desert landscape. Visitors can choose from a range of tour options, from short rides to multi-day expeditions.

Jeep tours are another popular way to explore the desert landscape, with tours available that take visitors to some of the most remote and beautiful areas of the desert. These tours often include stops at historic sites, such as the ancient city of Petra in Jordan.

Hot air balloon rides offer a unique perspective on the desert landscape, with breathtaking views of the mountains and valleys below. These rides are available in the Negev and Judean deserts, and are a popular activity for visitors looking for a once-in-a-lifetime experience.

Rock Climbing

Israel's diverse landscape offers a range of rock climbing opportunities, from the rocky cliffs of the Judean Desert to the limestone formations of the Galilee region. Some of the most popular rock climbing destinations in Israel include Ein Gedi, Ramon Crater, and the cliffs of Metzukei Dragot.

Ein Gedi is a nature reserve located in the Judean Desert, with stunning views of the Dead Sea and the surrounding mountains. The reserve offers a range of hiking trails and rock climbing routes, with options available for both beginners and experienced climbers.

Ramon Crater is a unique geological formation located in the Negev Desert, with towering cliffs and challenging rock climbing routes. The crater is a popular destination for outdoor enthusiasts, with a range of activities available, including hiking, rappelling, and mountain biking.

The cliffs of Metzukei Dragot are located in the Judean Desert, and offer some of the most challenging and rewarding rock climbing routes in Israel. The cliffs are known for their steep inclines and rugged terrain, and are a popular destination for experienced climbers.

Israel's diverse landscape offers a wide range of outdoor activities for visitors and locals alike. From hiking in the desert to swimming in the Mediterranean Sea, there is something for everyone to enjoy in Israel's great outdoors. Whether you're looking for an adrenaline-pumping adventure or a peaceful retreat in nature, Israel's outdoor activities are sure to satisfy.

Festivals and Events Throughout the Year

Israel is a land steeped in history and culture, with a rich tapestry of traditions and celebrations that have been passed down through the generations. Throughout the year, Israel is home to a wide variety of festivals and events that reflect this diversity, from religious festivals to cultural celebrations, music festivals to food fairs.

In this Guide, we will explore some of the most popular festivals and events that take place in Israel throughout the year.

January - March

In January, Israel celebrates the Jewish holiday of Tu B'Shvat, also known as the "New Year of Trees." This holiday marks the beginning of the agricultural cycle and is traditionally celebrated by planting trees and eating fruits and nuts. Many communities hold tree-planting events and nature walks to mark the occasion.

In February, Tel Aviv hosts its annual "Docaviv" documentary film festival. This festival brings together filmmakers and audiences from around the world to showcase some of the most compelling and thought-provoking documentaries of the year. With screenings held in venues throughout the city, Docaviv is a must-see event for film lovers.

March brings the annual Jerusalem Marathon, one of the biggest sporting events in Israel. The marathon attracts runners from around the world, who race through the streets of the ancient city, passing historic landmarks and breathtaking scenery along the way.

April - June

In April, Israel celebrates the Jewish holiday of Passover, a commemoration of the Exodus from Egypt. During this week-long festival, Jews around the world abstain from eating leavened bread and other leavened products. Many communities hold special Seders (ritual meals) to mark the holiday.

May brings the annual Israel Festival, a celebration of music, dance, theater, and visual arts. Held in venues throughout Jerusalem, the festival attracts performers from around the world, making it one of the most diverse and vibrant cultural events in the region.

June is the month of the Jerusalem Light Festival, a spectacular display of light and sound that illuminates the ancient city's landmarks and streets. The festival brings together artists and designers from around the world to create stunning visual installations that transform the city's architecture into a canvas for artistic expression.

July - September

In July, Israel celebrates the annual Karmiel Dance Festival, one of the largest dance festivals in the world. Held in the northern city of Karmiel, the festival attracts thousands of dancers and spectators, who come together to celebrate the art of dance in all its forms.

August is the month of the Tisha B'Av fast, a day of mourning and reflection for the Jewish people. On this day, Jews commemorate the destruction of the First and Second Temples in Jerusalem, as well as other tragic events in Jewish history. Many communities hold special prayer services and fasting to mark the occasion.

September brings the annual Tel Aviv White Night Festival, a celebration of art, music, and culture that takes place throughout the city's streets and public spaces. The festival kicks off at sundown and continues until dawn, with performances, exhibitions, and other cultural events held throughout the night.

October - December

In October, Israel celebrates the Jewish holiday of Sukkot, a harvest festival that commemorates the Israelites' journey through the desert. During this week-long festival, Jews build and decorate outdoor sukkahs (temporary shelters) and celebrate with meals, songs, and prayers.

November is the month of the annual Docaviv Negev Documentary Film Festival, held in the southern city of Sderot. This festival brings together filmmakers and audiences from around the world to showcase some of the most compelling and thought-provoking documentaries of the year.

December brings the annual Hanukkah festival, also known as the Festival of Lights. This eight-day holiday commemorates the rededication of the Second Temple in Jerusalem after its desecration by the Greeks. Jews around the world celebrate Hanukkah by lighting candles on a menorah, playing with dreidels, and eating foods fried in oil, such as latkes and sufganiyot.

In addition to these traditional Jewish holidays and events, Israel is also home to a wide variety of secular festivals and events throughout the year. Some of the most popular of these include:

1. The Red Sea Jazz Festival - Held annually in the southern city of Eilat, the Red Sea Jazz Festival is one of the largest and most prestigious jazz festivals in the world. The festival attracts top jazz musicians from around the world and features a diverse range of performances, workshops, and other events.

2. The Jerusalem Beer Festival - Held annually in the summer, the Jerusalem Beer Festival is a celebration of Israel's thriving craft beer scene. The festival brings together brewers from across the country to showcase their latest creations, and features live music, food stalls, and other attractions.

3. The Tel Aviv Pride Parade - Held annually in June, the Tel Aviv Pride Parade is one of the largest and most vibrant Pride events in the world. The parade attracts tens of thousands of participants and spectators from around the world, who come together to celebrate diversity and equality.

4. The Dead Sea Swim - Held annually in November, the Dead Sea Swim is a unique open-water swimming event that takes place in the saltiest body of water in the world. Participants can choose to swim either a 1.2-kilometer or 3.8-kilometer route, and are treated

to stunning views of the Dead Sea's mineral-rich waters.

5. The Eilat Birds Festival - Held annually in the southern city of Eilat, the Eilat Birds Festival is a celebration of Israel's rich birdlife. The festival brings together birdwatchers and nature enthusiasts from around the world to observe the migration of hundreds of bird species through the Eilat region.

6. The Jerusalem International Book Fair - Held every two years, the Jerusalem International Book Fair is one of the largest and most prestigious book fairs in the world. The fair brings together publishers, writers, and literary enthusiasts from around the world to showcase the latest books and ideas.

7. The Haifa International Film Festival - Held annually in the northern city of Haifa, the Haifa International Film Festival is a celebration of world

cinema. The festival showcases a wide range of international films, as well as Israeli and Palestinian films, and features screenings, discussions, and other events.

Israel is a land of vibrant cultural traditions and celebrations, with festivals and events taking place throughout the year. Whether you're interested in music, dance, theater, film, food, or outdoor activities, there is something for everyone in Israel's rich and diverse calendar of events. So why not plan a trip to Israel and experience the country's unique blend of history, culture, and celebration for yourself.

CHAPTER 6: JEWISH HERITAGE TRAVEL

Jewish heritage travel has become increasingly popular in recent years, as more and more people seek to explore their Jewish roots and learn about Jewish history and culture around the world. From ancient synagogues and historic Jewish neighborhoods to Holocaust memorials and Jewish museums, there are countless sites of significance for Jewish travelers to visit and explore.

One of the most popular destinations for Jewish heritage travel is Israel, which is home to a rich and diverse array of Jewish historical and cultural sites. From the ancient ruins of Masada and the Western Wall in Jerusalem to the vibrant contemporary Jewish culture of Tel Aviv, Israel is a fascinating destination for Jewish travelers looking to connect with their heritage.

Other popular destinations for Jewish heritage travel include Eastern Europe, where visitors can explore the remnants of the Jewish communities that thrived in places like Poland, Lithuania, and Hungary before being decimated by the Holocaust. The Jewish Museum in Berlin, Germany is another popular destination, as is the Anne Frank House in Amsterdam, which serves as a poignant reminder of the horrors of the Holocaust.

One of the unique aspects of Jewish heritage travel is the opportunity to connect with local Jewish communities and learn about contemporary Jewish life in different parts of the world. Whether it's attending a Shabbat service at a local synagogue, enjoying traditional Jewish foods at a local restaurant, or participating in cultural events and festivals, there are many ways to experience Jewish culture in different parts of the world.

In addition to the historical and cultural significance of Jewish heritage travel, there are also many spiritual and personal benefits to exploring one's Jewish roots. For many travelers, visiting Jewish historical sites and connecting with Jewish communities can be a deeply meaningful and transformative experience, helping them to deepen their connection to their Jewish identity and gain a greater appreciation for the richness and diversity of Jewish culture.

Whether you're a seasoned traveler or just starting to explore the world of Jewish heritage travel, there are many resources available to help you plan your trip and make the most of your experience. From guidebooks and online resources to organized tours and travel companies specializing in Jewish heritage travel, there are many ways to plan a trip that is tailored to your interests and needs.

Jewish heritage travel offers a unique and meaningful way to connect with Jewish history, culture, and identity around the world. Whether you're exploring ancient synagogues and Jewish neighborhoods in Israel, visiting Holocaust memorials and Jewish museums in Europe, or connecting with local Jewish communities in different parts of the world, there are countless opportunities to deepen your understanding and appreciation of Jewish heritage through travel. So why not plan your own Jewish heritage travel adventure and explore the rich and fascinating history and culture of the Jewish people.

Genealogy Resources and Services

Genealogy is the study and tracing of family lineages and history. It has become an increasingly popular hobby in recent years, as more and more people seek to learn about their ancestry and connect with their roots. Fortunately, there are many resources and services available to help people explore their family history, from online databases and research tools to professional genealogy services and DNA testing.

One of the most popular resources for genealogy research is ancestry.com, a subscription-based online platform that provides access to millions of historical records, including census data, military records, and immigration records. Ancestry.com also offers DNA testing services, which can provide valuable information about one's ancestry and help to connect individuals with relatives they may not have known existed.

Another popular online resource for genealogy research is familysearch.org, which provides free access to millions of historical records and other resources for genealogists. Familysearch.org is run by the Church of Jesus Christ of Latter-day Saints and is available to anyone who wants to explore their family history.

In addition to these online resources, there are also many professional genealogy services available to help individuals research their family history. These services can provide expert assistance with research and analysis, as well as access to specialized resources and databases. Some of the most well-known genealogy services include the National Genealogical Society and the Association of Professional Genealogists.

For individuals who are interested in DNA testing, there are also many companies that offer this service, including 23andMe, MyHeritage, and FamilyTreeDNA. DNA testing can provide valuable information about one's ancestry and can help to connect individuals with relatives they may not have known existed.

Another valuable resource for genealogy research is local libraries and archives. Many libraries and archives maintain extensive collections of historical records, including census data, military records, and immigration records. They can also provide access to specialized resources, such as local newspapers and historical maps.

In addition to these resources and services, there are also many genealogy societies and organizations that can provide valuable support and guidance to individuals who are interested in exploring their family history. These organizations often offer educational programs and workshops, as well as access to specialized resources and databases.

Genealogy research has become an increasingly popular hobby in recent years, as more and more people seek to learn about their ancestry and connect with their roots. Fortunately, there are many resources and services available to help individuals explore their family history, from online databases and research tools to professional genealogy services and DNA testing. Whether you're just starting to explore your family history or are a seasoned genealogist, there are many tools and resources available to help you uncover the fascinating history of your family lineage.

Jewish History Tours and Experiences

Jewish history tours and experiences offer a unique opportunity to explore the rich cultural and historical heritage of the Jewish people. These tours and experiences can be found in many parts of the world, including Israel, Europe, and the United States, and are designed to provide a deeper understanding of Jewish history and culture.

One of the most popular destinations for Jewish history tours is Israel, which is home to many significant historical and religious sites. Visitors to Israel can explore the ancient city of Jerusalem, which is home to the Western Wall, the Temple Mount, and many other important religious and historical sites. Other popular destinations in Israel include the Dead Sea, Masada, and the ancient city of Akko.

In addition to Israel, there are also many Jewish history tours available in Europe, which has a rich and diverse Jewish history. Visitors to Europe can explore the vibrant Jewish communities of cities such as Berlin, Budapest, and Prague, which are home to many synagogues, museums, and other cultural institutions.

Another popular destination for Jewish history tours is the United States, which is home to many historic Jewish communities and institutions. Visitors can explore the Jewish neighborhoods of cities such as New

York, Boston, and Los Angeles, which are home to many synagogues, museums, and other cultural institutions.

In addition to guided tours, there are also many Jewish history experiences available that offer a more immersive and interactive experience. These experiences can include hands-on workshops, cooking classes, and cultural performances, as well as opportunities to meet and interact with local Jewish communities.

One popular Jewish history experience is the annual Jewish cultural festival, which takes place in many cities around the world. These festivals offer a wide range of cultural activities, including live music performances, traditional food and drink, and arts and crafts.

Another popular Jewish history experience is the Jewish heritage tour, which provides a deeper understanding of Jewish culture and history. These tours can include visits to important historical and cultural sites, as well as opportunities to meet and interact with local Jewish communities.

In addition to these tours and experiences, there are also many online resources available for those interested in exploring Jewish history and culture. These resources can include online museums, virtual tours, and digital archives, as well as forums and discussion groups where individuals can connect and share information and experiences.

Jewish history tours and experiences offer a unique opportunity to explore the rich cultural and historical heritage of the Jewish people. Whether you're interested in exploring the ancient sites of Israel, the vibrant Jewish communities of Europe, or the historic Jewish neighborhoods of the United States, there are many tours and experiences available that can provide a deeper understanding of Jewish culture and history. Whether you're a seasoned traveler or a curious beginner, there are many tools and resources available to help you explore the fascinating history of the Jewish people.

Jewish Cultural Events and Festivals

Israel is home to many cultural events and festivals that celebrate the Jewish heritage and culture. These events are held throughout the year and offer visitors a unique opportunity to experience the vibrant Jewish culture and traditions of the country.

One of the most popular Jewish cultural events in Israel is the Jewish holiday of Passover, which takes place in the spring. Passover commemorates the liberation of the Jewish people from slavery in ancient Egypt and is celebrated with special prayers, traditional foods, and family gatherings. Many hotels and restaurants in Israel offer special Passover packages, and there are also many public events and activities that take place throughout the country.

Another popular Jewish cultural event in Israel is the festival of Purim, which takes place in late winter or early spring. Purim commemorates the salvation of the Jewish people from destruction in ancient Persia and is celebrated with costumes, parties, and traditional foods such as hamantaschen. In many cities in Israel, there are parades and public events that take place during Purim, and it is a festive time of year for Jews and non-Jews alike.

The Jewish holiday of Hanukkah, which takes place in December, is also widely celebrated in Israel. Hanukkah commemorates the miracle of the oil in the ancient temple in Jerusalem and is celebrated with the lighting of the menorah, traditional foods such as sufganiyot (jelly-filled donuts), and gift-giving. There are many public events and activities that take place during Hanukkah in Israel, including public menorah lightings, concerts, and markets.

In addition to these Jewish holidays, Israel is also home to many cultural events and festivals that celebrate Jewish arts, music, and literature. The Jerusalem International Book Fair is a popular event that takes place every two years and brings together writers, publishers, and literary agents from around the world. The Jerusalem Film Festival is another popular event that takes place every summer and showcases films from Israel and around the world.

The Israel Festival is a major cultural event that takes place every year in Jerusalem and features performances by artists and musicians from Israel and around the world. The festival includes a wide range of events, including theater, dance, music, and visual arts, and is a celebration of the diversity and creativity of Israeli culture.

Another popular Jewish cultural event in Israel is the Klezmer Festival, which takes place every August in Safed. The festival celebrates Jewish klezmer music, which originated in Eastern Europe, and features concerts, workshops, and other cultural events.

Israel is home to a rich and diverse Jewish culture, and there are many events and festivals throughout the year that celebrate this heritage. Whether you're interested in Jewish holidays and traditions, music and arts, or literature and film, there is something for everyone in Israel's vibrant Jewish cultural scene. These events provide a unique opportunity for visitors to experience the rich and diverse Jewish culture of Israel and to connect with the country's rich heritage and traditions.

CHAPTER 7: CHRISTIAN PILGRIMAGE SITES

Israel is not only a holy land for Jews but also for Christians, as it is home to many important Christian pilgrimage sites. These sites are significant for Christians as they are associated with the life and ministry of Jesus Christ, and visiting them is a way to deepen one's faith and connect with the history of Christianity.

Here are some of the most important Christian pilgrimage sites in Israel:

1. The Church of the Holy Sepulchre: Located in the Old City of Jerusalem, the Church of the Holy Sepulchre is believed to be the site where Jesus was crucified, buried, and resurrected. The church is one of the most important Christian pilgrimage sites in the world, and visitors can see the traditional sites of the crucifixion and burial of Jesus.

2. The Via Dolorosa: Also located in the Old City of Jerusalem, the Via Dolorosa is the traditional route that Jesus took on the way to his crucifixion. Visitors can walk the 14 stations of the cross, which mark important events along the way, including the place where Jesus met his mother and the spot where he was nailed to the cross.

3. The Sea of Galilee: Located in northern Israel, the Sea of Galilee is the site of many important events in the life of Jesus, including his walking

on water and his feeding of the 5,000. Visitors can take a boat ride on the sea and visit the nearby Mount of Beatitudes, where Jesus delivered his famous Sermon on the Mount.

4. The Mount of Olives: Located in Jerusalem, the Mount of Olives is believed to be the site where Jesus ascended to heaven. Visitors can also see the Church of All Nations, which is built on the site where Jesus prayed before his arrest.

5. Bethlehem: Located just outside of Jerusalem, Bethlehem is the birthplace of Jesus and is home to the Church of the Nativity, which is built on the site where Jesus was born.

6. Nazareth: Located in northern Israel, Nazareth is the childhood home of Jesus and is home to the Basilica of the Annunciation, which marks the spot where the angel Gabriel appeared to Mary and announced the birth of Jesus.

7.   Capernaum: Located on the shores of the Sea of Galilee, Capernaum was a fishing village where Jesus is said to have performed many miracles. Visitors can see the remains of the ancient village, including a synagogue that dates back to the time of Jesus.

8. Mount Tabor: Located in the Lower Galilee region of Israel, Mount Tabor is believed to be the site of the Transfiguration of Jesus. According to the Bible, Jesus ascended the mountain with three of his disciples, where he was transformed before their eyes. Today, visitors can climb to the top of the mountain and visit the Church of the Transfiguration, which was built in the 4th century.

9. Emmaus Nicopolis:

Emmaus Nicopolis is located in the Judean hills, about 20 km west of Jerusalem. This site is associated with the appearance of the risen Jesus to his disciples on the road to Emmaus. According to the Gospel of Luke, Jesus appeared to two of his disciples on the road to Emmaus, but they did not recognize him until he broke bread with them. Visitors to Emmaus Nicopolis can see the remains of an ancient city, including a Roman amphitheater and a Crusader church.

10.   Mount Carmel:

Mount Carmel is located in northern Israel, near the city of Haifa. This mountain is associated with the prophet Elijah, who is said to have defeated the prophets of the god Baal in a contest on the mountain. Today, visitors can visit the Cave of Elijah, which is located on the mountain and is believed to be the spot where Elijah hid from King Ahab and Queen Jezebel.

11. Jericho:

Jericho is located in the Jordan Valley, near the Dead Sea. This ancient city is associated with several important events in the life of Jesus, including his healing of the blind man Bartimaeus and his meeting with the tax collector Zacchaeus. Visitors to Jericho can also see the remains of the ancient city, including the walls that were destroyed by Joshua during the conquest of Canaan.

12. Tel Megiddo:

Tel Megiddo is an ancient city that is located in northern Israel, near the modern city of Afula. This site is associated with the Book of Revelation, which describes a final battle between good and evil at a place called Armageddon. Tel Megiddo is believed to be the site of the ancient city of Megiddo, which was destroyed and rebuilt several times over the centuries.

Visiting these Christian pilgrimage sites is a way for believers to deepen their faith and connect with the history of Christianity. Many visitors find that their visit to Israel is a life-changing experience that strengthens their faith and provides a deeper understanding of the Christian religion.

Biblical Sites and Landmarks

Israel is home to many important biblical sites and landmarks, some of which are considered sacred by Jews, Christians, and Muslims alike. Here are some of the most significant biblical sites and landmarks in Israel:

1. Jerusalem: This city is holy to Jews, Christians, and Muslims, and is considered the site of many important biblical events, including the building of the First and Second Temples, the crucifixion and resurrection of Jesus Christ, and the ascension of the Prophet Muhammad.

2. The Western Wall: This is the last remaining part of the Second Temple, and is considered one of the holiest sites in Judaism. Many Jews come to the Western Wall to pray and leave written prayers in the cracks between the stones.

3. The Dome of the Rock: This is a Muslim shrine located on the Temple Mount in Jerusalem. It is believed to be the site of the Prophet Muhammad's ascent to heaven, and is considered one of the holiest sites in Islam.

4. The Church of the Holy Sepulchre: This is a Christian church located in Jerusalem that is believed to be the site of Jesus Christ's crucifixion, burial, and resurrection.

5. The Sea of Galilee: This is a freshwater lake in northern Israel that is mentioned in the New Testament as the site of many of Jesus Christ's

miracles, including walking on water and calming a storm.

6. The Mount of Olives: This is a hill located in Jerusalem that is mentioned in the Bible as the site of many important events, including Jesus Christ's final ascent to heaven and his betrayal by Judas.

7. The Garden of Gethsemane: This is a garden located at the foot of the Mount of Olives in Jerusalem that is mentioned in the Bible as the site where Jesus Christ prayed before his arrest and crucifixion.

8. The Dead Sea: This is a saltwater lake located in the Jordan Rift Valley that is mentioned in the Bible as the site of the destruction of Sodom and Gomorrah, and is believed to have healing properties.

9. Masada: This is a fortress located on a mountain in the Judean Desert that is mentioned in the Bible as the site of a

Jewish revolt against the Roman Empire.

10. Bethlehem: This is a city located near Jerusalem that is believed to be the birthplace of Jesus Christ, and is home to the Church of the Nativity.

11. Nazareth: This is a city in northern Israel that is believed to be the childhood home of Jesus Christ, and is home to the Basilica of the Annunciation, which commemorates the announcement of Jesus' birth to the Virgin Mary.

12. Mount Sinai: This is a mountain in the Sinai Peninsula that is mentioned in the Old Testament as the site where Moses received the Ten Commandments from God.

13. Jericho: This is a city located in the West Bank that is mentioned in the Bible as the site of the Israelites' conquest of the Promised Land.

14. Hebron: This is a city in the West Bank that is mentioned in the Bible as

the burial place of the patriarchs Abraham, Isaac, and Jacob.

15. Caesarea: This is an ancient Roman city located on the coast of Israel that is mentioned in the New Testament as the site where the Apostle Peter converted the Roman centurion Cornelius to Christianity.

16. Megiddo: This is an archaeological site located in northern Israel that is mentioned in the Bible as the site of several battles, including the final battle of Armageddon.

17. Mount Tabor: This is a mountain in northern Israel that is mentioned in the Bible as the site of the Transfiguration, where Jesus was seen in his divine glory by his disciples.

18. Capernaum: This is a fishing village located on the shore of the Sea of Galilee that is mentioned in the New Testament as the site of several of Jesus Christ's miracles.

19.Mount Carmel: This is a mountain range in northern Israel that is mentioned in the Old Testament as the site of the prophet Elijah's showdown with the prophets of the pagan god Baal.

20. Qumran: This is an archaeological site located near the Dead Sea that is famous for the discovery of the Dead Sea Scrolls, which contain some of the earliest known copies of the Hebrew Bible.

Israel is home to many important biblical sites and landmarks that are significant to Jews, Christians, and Muslims. These sites range from ancient ruins and archaeological sites to cities and natural wonders, and each has its own unique history and significance. Visiting these sites can provide a deeper understanding and appreciation for the religious and cultural history of the region, and they continue to be important pilgrimage destinations for people of faith around the world.

Christian Holy Land Tours and Experiences

Christian holy land tours in Israel offer a unique opportunity to explore and experience the biblical sites and landmarks that are significant to Christianity. Here are some of the most popular Christian holy land tours and experiences in Israel:

1. Walking Tour of Jerusalem: This tour takes you through the Old City of Jerusalem, visiting the Western Wall, the Church of the Holy Sepulchre, and other important sites.

2. Tour of the Via Dolorosa: This tour retraces the path that Jesus took through the streets of Jerusalem on the way to his crucifixion, stopping at each of the 14 stations of the cross.

3. Visit to Bethlehem: This tour takes you to the birthplace of Jesus Christ, including a visit to the Church of the Nativity.

4. Boat Tour of the Sea of Galilee: This tour takes you out onto the Sea of Galilee, where you can experience the same waters that Jesus walked on and performed miracles on.
5. Mount of Olives Tour: This tour takes you to the Mount of Olives, where you can visit the Garden of Gethsemane and the Church of All Nations.
6. Qumran Tour: This tour takes you to the site where the Dead Sea Scrolls were discovered, providing a fascinating insight into the history of Judaism and early Christianity.
7. Masada and Dead Sea Tour: This tour takes you to the ancient fortress of Masada, followed by a visit to the Dead Sea, where you can float in the salty waters and enjoy the healing properties of the mud.
8. Christian Galilee Tour: This tour takes you to the beautiful landscapes of the Galilee region, visiting Christian holy sites such as the Mount of Beatitudes

and the Church of the Multiplication of the Loaves and Fishes.

9. Nazareth Tour: This tour takes you to the hometown of Jesus, where you can visit the Basilica of the Annunciation and other important Christian sites.

10. Golan Heights Tour: This tour takes you to the Golan Heights, where you can explore the natural beauty of the area and learn about the history of the region, including the Syrian-Israeli conflict.

These Christian holy land tours and experiences offer a unique opportunity to deepen your faith and understanding of the Bible, and to explore the rich cultural and historical heritage of Israel.

Christian Religious Events and Festivals

Israel hosts several Christian religious events and festivals throughout the year, attracting thousands of pilgrims and tourists from all over the world. Here are some of the most important Christian religious events and festivals in Israel:

1. Easter: Easter is the most important Christian holiday, commemorating the crucifixion and resurrection of Jesus Christ. In Israel, there are special Easter celebrations and processions in Jerusalem, including the Holy Fire ceremony at the Church of the Holy Sepulchre.

2. Christmas: Christmas is a major Christian holiday, celebrating the birth of Jesus Christ. In Israel, there are special Christmas celebrations and processions in Bethlehem, including Midnight Mass at the Church of the Nativity.

3. Palm Sunday: Palm Sunday is a Christian holiday that marks the beginning of Holy Week, commemorating Jesus' triumphal entry into Jerusalem. In Israel, there is a special Palm Sunday procession

from the Mount of Olives to the Old City of Jerusalem.

4. Pentecost: Pentecost is a Christian holiday that commemorates the descent of the Holy Spirit upon the apostles. In Israel, there are special Pentecost celebrations in the Church of the Holy Sepulchre and other Christian holy sites.

5. Feast of the Transfiguration: The Feast of the Transfiguration is a Christian holiday that celebrates the Transfiguration of Jesus on Mount Tabor. In Israel, there is a special celebration at the Church of the Transfiguration on Mount Tabor.

6. Feast of the Assumption: The Feast of the Assumption is a Christian holiday that celebrates the ascent of the Virgin Mary into heaven. In Israel, there is a special celebration at the Church of the Dormition in Jerusalem.

7. Feast of Saint George: The Feast of Saint George is a Christian holiday

that commemorates the martyrdom of Saint George. In Israel, there is a special celebration at the Greek Orthodox Monastery of Saint George in Lod.

8. Feast of Saint John the Baptist: The Feast of Saint John the Baptist is a Christian holiday that commemorates the birth of John the Baptist. In Israel, there is a special celebration at the Church of St. John the Baptist in Ein Kerem.

These Christian religious events and festivals offer a unique opportunity to experience the rich cultural and historical heritage of Christianity in Israel, and to participate in the celebrations and traditions of the Christian faith.

CHAPTER 8: MUSLIM HERITAGE SITES

Israel is home to several important Muslim heritage sites, many of which are located in Jerusalem. Here are some of the most significant Muslim heritage sites in Israel:

1. Al-Aqsa Mosque: Al-Aqsa Mosque is one of the holiest sites in Islam, located on the Temple Mount in Jerusalem. It is believed to be the site from which the Prophet Muhammad ascended to heaven during his Night Journey.

2. Dome of the Rock: The Dome of the Rock is a shrine located on the Temple Mount in Jerusalem, believed to mark the spot where the Prophet Muhammad ascended to heaven. It is also believed to be the site of the Second Temple.

3. Old City of Jerusalem: The Old City of Jerusalem is home to several important Muslim heritage sites, including the Al-Aqsa Mosque, the Dome of the Rock, and the Western Wall.

4. Hebron: Hebron is an important city in Islamic history, believed to be the burial place of the Prophet Abraham and his family.

5. Al-Buraq Wall: The Al-Buraq Wall is located on the western side of the Temple Mount in Jerusalem, and is believed to be the spot where the Prophet Muhammad tied his magical steed, Buraq, during his Night Journey.

6. Cave of the Patriarchs: The Cave of the Patriarchs is located in the city of Hebron, and is believed to be the burial place of the Prophet Abraham and his family.

7. Haram al-Sharif: Haram al-Sharif, also known as the Noble Sanctuary, is a complex of Muslim heritage sites located on the Temple Mount in Jerusalem. It includes the Al-Aqsa Mosque and the Dome of the Rock, among other sites.

8. Nabi Musa: Nabi Musa is a mosque located in the Judean Desert, believed to be the burial place of the Prophet Moses.

These Muslim heritage sites in Israel offer a rich history and cultural significance for Muslims around the world. Visiting these sites can provide a deeper understanding and appreciation for the Islamic faith and its heritage in Israel.

Islamic Holy Sites and Landmarks

There are several Islamic holy sites and landmarks in Israel, many of which are located in Jerusalem. Here are some of the most important Islamic holy sites and landmarks in Israel:

1. Al-Aqsa Mosque: Al-Aqsa Mosque is one of the holiest sites in Islam, located on the Temple Mount in Jerusalem. It is considered the third holiest site in Islam after Mecca and Medina, and is believed to be the site where the Prophet Muhammad ascended to heaven during his Night Journey.

2. Dome of the Rock: The Dome of the Rock is a shrine located on the Temple Mount in Jerusalem, believed to mark the spot where the Prophet Muhammad ascended to heaven. It is also believed to be the site of the Second Temple.

3. Old City of Jerusalem: The Old City of Jerusalem is home to several important Islamic sites, including the Al-Aqsa Mosque, the Dome of the Rock, and the Western Wall.
4. Hebron: Hebron is an important city in Islamic history, believed to be the burial place of the Prophet Abraham and his family.
5. Masjid al-Khalil: Masjid al-Khalil, also known as the Ibrahimi Mosque, is located in Hebron and is believed to be the burial place of the Prophet Abraham and his family.
6. Masjid al-Jazzar: Masjid al-Jazzar is located in the city of Acre and is one of the largest mosques in Israel.
7. Masjid al-Basha: Masjid al-Basha is located in the city of Tiberias and was built by the Ottoman governor of the city in the 18th century.
8. Nabi Musa: Nabi Musa is a mosque located in the Judean Desert, believed

to be the burial place of the Prophet Moses.

These Islamic holy sites and landmarks in Israel offer a unique opportunity to experience the rich cultural and historical heritage of Islam in the region. They are also important pilgrimage sites for Muslims around the world.

Muslim Cultural Events and Festivals

As a predominantly Muslim country, Israel has several cultural events and festivals that are celebrated by the Muslim population. Some of these include:

1. Eid al-Fitr: This is the festival of breaking the fast, which marks the end of Ramadan, the holy month of fasting. It is celebrated for three days and is a time of family gatherings, feasting, and gift-giving.
2. Eid al-Adha: This is the festival of sacrifice, which marks the end of the annual Hajj pilgrimage to Mecca. It is

celebrated for three days and involves the sacrifice of an animal, usually a sheep or a goat, to commemorate the willingness of Prophet Ibrahim (Abraham) to sacrifice his son Ismail (Ishmael) as an act of obedience to God.

3. Mawlid al-Nabi: This is the celebration of the birthday of the Prophet Muhammad, which is marked on the 12th day of Rabi' al-awwal, the third month of the Islamic calendar. It is a time for Muslims to remember the life and teachings of the Prophet Muhammad.

4. Laylat al-Qadr: This is the Night of Power, which is believed to be the night when the first verses of the Quran were revealed to the Prophet Muhammad. It is observed on the 27th night of Ramadan and is considered to be the holiest night of the year.

5. Al-Isra' wal-Mi'raj: This is the Night Journey and Ascension of the Prophet

Muhammad, which is believed to have occurred on the 27th day of Rajab, the seventh month of the Islamic calendar. It is a time for Muslims to remember the spiritual journey of the Prophet Muhammad from Mecca to Jerusalem and then to heaven.

These are some of the major Muslim cultural events and festivals that are celebrated in Israel.

Halal Dining and Prayer Accommodations

Israel is a country that caters to diverse religious and cultural needs, including those of Muslims. Here are some options for halal dining and prayer accommodations in Israel:

Halal Dining:

1. Abu Hassan - A popular hummus restaurant located in Jaffa, Tel Aviv,

that serves halal meat and vegetarian options.

2. Falafel Bashir - A popular falafel restaurant in Nazareth that serves halal meat and vegetarian options.
3. Al-Fahham - A family-owned restaurant in Nazareth that serves halal meat and Middle Eastern dishes.
4. Al-Baba Sweets - A dessert shop in Haifa that serves halal sweets, such as baklava and Turkish delight.

Prayer Accommodations:

1. Al-Aqsa Mosque - Located in Jerusalem's Old City, Al-Aqsa Mosque is the third holiest site in Islam and welcomes Muslim worshippers.
2. Masjid Al-Jazzar - A mosque in Akko (Acre) that dates back to the Ottoman era and welcomes Muslim worshippers.
3. Masjid al-Omari - A mosque in Bethlehem that dates back to the 13th

century and welcomes Muslim worshippers.

4. Masjid al-Anwar - A mosque in Nazareth that dates back to the 18th century and welcomes Muslim worshippers.

Additionally, many hotels in Israel offer halal dining options and prayer accommodations for their Muslim guests. It is always recommended to inquire in advance about these options to ensure a comfortable stay.

CHAPTER 9:
OFF-THE-BEATEN-PATH
DESTINATIONS

Israel is a land of diverse culture, history, and landscapes, offering something for everyone, from the ancient cities to modern towns, from desert landscapes to lush green mountains. While Jerusalem, Tel Aviv, and the Dead Sea are popular tourist destinations, there are several off-the-beaten-path destinations that are worth exploring. These destinations offer unique experiences and are less crowded, allowing for a more intimate and authentic travel experience. In this Guide, we will explore some of the hidden gems of Israel that are waiting to be discovered.

1. Mount Tabor

Mount Tabor is a scenic mountain in the Lower Galilee region of Israel. The mountain is believed to be the site of the Transfiguration of Jesus, according to

Christian tradition. It is also an important site for Jewish and Muslim traditions. The mountain offers stunning panoramic views of the surrounding valleys and is home to several hiking trails. The hiking trails range from easy to difficult, catering to hikers of all skill levels. The most popular trail is the Jesus Trail, which is a 65 km trek from Nazareth to Capernaum. The trail passes through several historic sites, including Mount Tabor.

2. Ein Gedi Nature Reserve

Ein Gedi Nature Reserve is a desert oasis located on the eastern shore of the Dead Sea. The reserve is home to several waterfalls, pools, and hot springs, making it an ideal destination for nature lovers. The reserve is also home to several species of wildlife, including ibexes and hyraxes. The reserve offers several hiking trails, ranging from easy to difficult, catering to hikers of all skill levels. The most popular trail is the Nahal David Trail, which takes visitors through the reserve's stunning waterfalls and pools.

3. Akko

Akko (Acre) is a historic city located on the northern coast of Israel. The city is a UNESCO World Heritage Site and is home to several historic sites, including the Crusader Fortress, the Knights' Halls, and the Turkish Baths. The city also has a vibrant Arab market, where visitors can buy traditional handicrafts and taste local delicacies. The city's picturesque port and ancient walls make it an ideal destination for history and architecture enthusiasts.

4. Rosh Hanikra

Rosh Hanikra is a coastal grotto located on the northernmost tip of Israel, near the Lebanese border. The grotto is formed by the collision of the Mediterranean Sea and the cliffs, resulting in stunning natural arches and caves. The grotto can be reached by cable car, offering visitors a stunning view of the Mediterranean Sea. The grotto is also home to several hiking trails, offering stunning views of the sea and the surrounding cliffs.

5. Beit She'an National Park

Beit She'an National Park is an archaeological site located in the northern Jordan Valley. The site is home to several ruins, including a Roman amphitheater, a bathhouse, and a marketplace. The site also has a museum that showcases the history and culture of the region. The site is an ideal destination for history and archaeology enthusiasts.

6. Timna Park

Timna Park is a desert park located in southern Israel. The park is home to several geological formations, including sandstone cliffs and unique rock formations. The park also has several hiking trails, catering to hikers of all skill levels. The most popular trail is the Solomon's Pillars Trail, which takes visitors through the park's stunning rock formations.

7. Beit Guvrin-Maresha National Park

Beit Guvrin-Maresha National Park is an archaeological site located in central Israel. The site is home to several ruins, including an ancient city, a Roman amphitheater, and a network of underground caves and tunnels. The park also has several hiking trails, offering visitors the opportunity to explore the park's stunning landscapes. The underground caves and tunnels, known as the Bell Caves, are a unique feature of the park and are believed to have been used for quarrying in ancient times.

8. Haifa

Haifa is a coastal city located in northern Israel. The city is known for its stunning views of the Mediterranean Sea and its beautiful gardens. The city's most famous attraction is the Baha'i Gardens, a UNESCO World Heritage Site and one of the world's most visited gardens. The gardens offer stunning views of the city and the sea and are an ideal destination for nature and architecture enthusiasts. The city also has several museums and historic sites, including the Elijah's Cave and the Haifa Museum of Art.

9. Nimrod Fortress

Nimrod Fortress is a historic castle located in the Golan Heights region of Israel. The fortress was built in the 13th century by the Ayyubid dynasty and is one of the best-preserved medieval castles in the region. The fortress offers stunning views of the surrounding valleys and is an ideal destination for history and architecture enthusiasts.

10.   Zichron Ya'akov

Zichron Ya'akov is a picturesque town located on the coast of the Mediterranean Sea. The town is known for its beautiful gardens, historic houses, and wineries. The town's most famous attraction is the Baron's Rothschild's Estate, a UNESCO World Heritage Site and one of the finest examples of 19th-century architecture in the region. The estate is home to several gardens, including a rose garden and a palm garden, and is an ideal destination for nature and architecture enthusiasts.

11. Caesarea National Park

Caesarea National Park is an archaeological site located on the coast of the Mediterranean Sea. The site is home to several ruins, including an ancient city, a Roman amphitheater, and a harbor. The site also has a museum that showcases the history and culture of the region. The site is an ideal destination for history and archaeology enthusiasts.

12. Ein Hod

Ein Hod is a picturesque artist village located on the coast of the Mediterranean Sea. The village is home to several galleries and studios, showcasing the works of local artists. The village also has several restaurants and cafes, offering visitors the opportunity to taste local delicacies. The village's beautiful gardens and scenic views make it an ideal destination for nature and art enthusiasts.

Israel is a country that offers something for everyone, from the ancient cities to modern towns, from desert landscapes to lush green mountains. While the popular tourist destinations are worth exploring, there are several off-the-beaten-path destinations that are waiting to be discovered. These destinations offer unique experiences and are less crowded, allowing for a more intimate and authentic travel experience. From the desert oasis of Ein Gedi to the historic city of Akko, Israel's hidden gems are waiting to be explored.

Hidden Gems and Lesser-Known Destinations

Israel is a small country with a rich history and diverse cultural heritage, which makes it an excellent destination for tourists who want to experience something unique and off the beaten path. While many visitors flock to popular sites such as Jerusalem, Tel Aviv, and the Dead Sea, there are many hidden gems and lesser-known destinations that are worth exploring. From ancient ruins to natural wonders, here are some of the hidden gems and lesser-known destinations in Israel.

1. Beit Guvrin National Park

Beit Guvrin National Park is located in the Judean Lowlands in central Israel and is home to a vast network of ancient caves and underground tunnels that date back to the time of the Maccabees. The park covers an area of over 5,000 acres and is home to thousands of caves, many of which are still being explored by archaeologists. Visitors can take a guided tour of the park and explore the caves, which were used for everything from burial sites to hideouts for Jewish rebels during the Roman occupation.

2. The Baha'i Gardens

The Baha'i Gardens are a series of terraced gardens located in Haifa, Israel. They were designed and built by the Baha'i faith, which is a monotheistic religion that originated in Iran in the mid-19th century. The gardens cover an area of over 19 acres and are home to a variety of plants and flowers from around the world. Visitors can take a guided tour of the gardens and learn about the Baha'i faith and its principles of unity, equality, and peace.

3. Mount Tabor

Mount Tabor is a mountain located in the Lower Galilee region of Israel. It is considered to be one of the holiest sites in the Christian religion and is believed to be the site of the Transfiguration of Jesus. Visitors can hike to the top of the mountain and take in the stunning views of the surrounding countryside. There are also several churches and monasteries located on the mountain, including the Church of the Transfiguration, which was built in the 4th century.

4. Timna Park

Timna Park is located in the southern part of Israel and is home to a stunning collection of natural rock formations and ancient copper mines. The park covers an area of over 60 square miles and is home to several hiking trails, including the Red Canyon trail, which takes visitors through a narrow canyon with towering red rock walls. Visitors can also take a guided tour of the ancient copper mines and learn about the history of mining in the region.

5. Rosh Hanikra

Rosh Hanikra is a natural grotto located on the Mediterranean coast of Israel, near the border with Lebanon. The grotto is formed by the erosion of soft rock by the sea and is home to a series of underground caves and tunnels. Visitors can take a cable car down to the grotto and explore the caves and tunnels on foot. The area is also home to a variety of marine life, including sea turtles and dolphins.

6. The Crusader Fortress of Akko

The Crusader Fortress of Akko is located in the city of Acre (also known as Akko) in northern Israel. The fortress was built by the Crusaders in the 12th century and was one of the most important strongholds of the Crusader Kingdom of Jerusalem. Visitors can explore the fortress and learn about its history, which includes sieges by Muslim armies and the imprisonment of the Knights Templar.

7. The Dead Sea Scrolls at the Israel Museum

The Israel Museum in Jerusalem is home to one of the most important collections of ancient artifacts in the world, including the Dead Sea Scrolls. The scrolls are a collection of Jewish texts that date back to the Second Temple period (approximately 200 BCE to 70 CE) and were discovered in the caves of Qumran near the Dead Sea in the 1940s and 1950s. The museum has a dedicated exhibit that showcases some of the most important scrolls, including the Great Isaiah Scroll, which is the largest and most complete of the Dead Sea Scrolls.

8. The Ramon Crater

The Ramon Crater, also known as Makhtesh Ramon, is a geological formation located in the Negev Desert in southern Israel. The crater is approximately 40 km long and 10 km wide and is the largest of its kind in the world. Visitors can explore the crater on foot or by bike and take in the stunning views of the desert landscape. The area is also home to several unique species of desert wildlife, including ibexes and hyraxes.

9. The city of Safed

Safed, also known as Tzfat, is a small city located in northern Israel. It is one of the four holy cities in Judaism and is known for its rich history and vibrant art scene. The city is home to several synagogues and yeshivas, including the Ari Ashkenazi Synagogue, which is named after Rabbi Isaac Luria, a 16th-century mystic who lived in Safed. Visitors can also explore the city's many art galleries and workshops, which showcase the work of local artists and craftsmen.

10. The Ein Gedi Nature Reserve

The Ein Gedi Nature Reserve is located on the eastern shore of the Dead Sea and is home to a variety of rare plants and animals, including the Nubian ibex and the rock hyrax. Visitors can explore the reserve on foot and take in the stunning views of the surrounding desert landscape. The area is also home to several natural hot springs, which are said to have healing properties.

11. The City of David

The City of David is an archaeological site located in the ancient city of Jerusalem. It is believed to be the site of the original settlement that King David established when he captured the city from the Jebusites in the 10th century BCE. Visitors can explore the site and see the remains of the city walls, fortifications, and buildings. The site also includes a water tunnel that was built during the reign of King Hezekiah in the 8th century BCE.

12. The White Mosque of Ramla

The White Mosque of Ramla is a unique example of early Islamic architecture and is located in the city of Ramla in central Israel. The mosque was built in the 8th century and is one of the oldest and best-preserved examples of early Islamic architecture in the region. Visitors can explore the mosque and learn about its history, which includes periods of use as a mosque, a church, and a prison.

13. The Ayalon Institute

The Ayalon Institute is a former clandestine ammunition factory located in central Israel. It was established by Jewish fighters during the British Mandate period and played a crucial role in supplying weapons and ammunition to Jewish paramilitary groups in the lead-up to the establishment of the State of Israel. Visitors can take a guided tour of the site and learn about the history of the underground movement that operated there.

14. The Mount of Olives

The Mount of Olives is a mountain ridge located east of the Old City of Jerusalem. It is one of the most important sites in the

Jewish and Christian religions and is believed to be the site of several important events in the life of Jesus, including his ascension to heaven. Visitors can take in the stunning views of the Old City and visit several important religious sites, including the Church of All Nations and the Garden of Gethsemane.

15. The Western Wall Tunnel

The Western Wall Tunnel is an underground tunnel that runs along the length of the Western Wall, which is one of the holiest sites in Judaism. The tunnel provides visitors with a unique perspective on the history of the site and allows them to see the massive stones that make up the Western Wall up close. The tunnel also includes several archaeological exhibits that showcase the history of the site, including the remains of a Roman road that once ran through the area.

16. The Beit Guvrin-Maresha National Park

The Beit Guvrin-Maresha National Park is located in central Israel and is home to a series of underground caves and tunnels that were carved out by the ancient inhabitants of the area. The caves were used for a variety of purposes, including as burial sites, storage facilities, and even as underground pigeon coops. Visitors can explore the caves and tunnels and see the incredible artwork and inscriptions that have been preserved there.

17. The Red Sea Coral Reef Reserve

The Red Sea Coral Reef Reserve is located off the coast of Eilat in southern Israel and is home to some of the most beautiful and diverse coral reefs in the world. The reserve is a popular destination for snorkeling and diving and allows visitors to see a wide variety of marine life, including colorful fish, dolphins, and even sea turtles. The reserve is also home to several shipwrecks that provide a unique diving experience.

18.   The Mount Carmel National Park

The Mount Carmel National Park is located in northern Israel and is home to a diverse range of flora and fauna. The park is a popular destination for hiking and includes several scenic trails that offer stunning views of the surrounding landscape. Visitors can also explore the park's many caves and learn about the area's rich history, which includes periods of occupation by ancient civilizations.

19. The Rosh Hanikra Grottoes

The Rosh Hanikra Grottoes are a series of sea caves located on the border between Israel and Lebanon. The caves are formed from limestone and have been eroded by the waves of the Mediterranean Sea over thousands of years. Visitors can explore the caves and take in the stunning views of the sea and the surrounding landscape. The area is also home to several rare species of flora and fauna.

20.   The Bahá'í Gardens in Haifa

The Bahá'í Gardens in Haifa are a series of terraced gardens that are located on the slope of Mount Carmel. The gardens are a UNESCO World Heritage site and are considered one of the most beautiful sights in Israel. Visitors can take a guided tour of the gardens and learn about the history and beliefs of the Bahá'í faith. The gardens also provide stunning views of the city of Haifa and the Mediterranean Sea.

Israel is a country with a rich and diverse history, and there are countless hidden gems and lesser-known destinations that offer visitors a unique and unforgettable experience.

Unique Cultural Experiences

Israel is a country that is steeped in history, culture, and tradition. Its unique cultural experiences are a result of the country's rich history, which dates back thousands of years. Israel is the birthplace of Judaism, Christianity, and Islam, and the country has been home to a diverse range of cultures, religions, and ethnicities throughout its history. As a result, Israel offers a unique cultural experience that is unlike anything else in the world. In this Guide, we will explore some of the unique cultural experiences that Israel has to offer.

Jerusalem: A Spiritual and Cultural Center

Jerusalem is one of the most important spiritual and cultural centers in the world. It is the birthplace of three major religions: Judaism, Christianity, and Islam. The city is home to many important religious sites, including the Western Wall, the Church of the Holy Sepulchre, and the Dome of the Rock. Each of these sites has a unique cultural and spiritual significance, and they are a testament to the city's rich history and diverse cultural heritage.

In addition to its religious significance, Jerusalem is also a cultural hub. The city is home to many museums, galleries, and cultural institutions, including the Israel Museum, the Jerusalem Theatre, and the Yad Vashem Holocaust Museum. These institutions offer visitors a glimpse into the country's rich cultural history and provide a deeper understanding of the complex issues that have shaped the region.

Tel Aviv: A Modern and Vibrant City

Tel Aviv is Israel's largest city and one of the most vibrant and cosmopolitan cities in the world. The city is known for its modern architecture, stunning beaches, and thriving arts and culture scene. Tel Aviv is a city that never sleeps, with a bustling nightlife and a wide range of restaurants, cafes, and bars.

One of the unique cultural experiences that Tel Aviv has to offer is its street art scene. The city is home to many talented street artists who have transformed the city's walls and buildings into works of art. The street art scene in Tel Aviv is constantly evolving, with new works of art popping up all the time.

In addition to its street art scene, Tel Aviv is also home to many museums, galleries, and cultural institutions, including the Tel Aviv Museum of Art, the Israeli Opera, and the Cameri Theatre. These institutions offer visitors a glimpse into the city's rich cultural heritage and provide a deeper understanding of the issues that have shaped the city.

The Dead Sea: A Natural Wonder

The Dead Sea is one of Israel's most unique natural wonders. The sea is located at the lowest point on earth and is known for its high salt concentration, which makes it impossible for swimmers to sink. The mineral-rich mud found in the sea is also believed to have therapeutic properties, and many visitors come to the Dead Sea to experience its healing effects.

The Dead Sea is surrounded by stunning natural scenery, including the Masada National Park and the Ein Gedi Nature Reserve. These areas offer visitors the opportunity to explore the region's unique flora and fauna and to experience the beauty of the desert landscape.

The Bedouin Culture: A Nomadic Way of Life

The Bedouin people are a nomadic group that has inhabited the deserts of the Middle East for thousands of years. The Bedouin way of life is centered around the concept of hospitality, and visitors to Israel have the opportunity to experience this unique culture firsthand.

One of the most popular ways to experience Bedouin culture is through a visit to a Bedouin camp. These camps offer visitors the opportunity to spend a night in a traditional Bedouin tent, to enjoy traditional Bedouin food, and to learn about the Bedouin way of life. Visitors can also go on a camel ride through the desert and explore the unique landscape of the region.

The Bedouin people are also known for their traditional crafts, such as weaving and embroidery. Visitors can purchase handmade Bedouin crafts and souvenirs at markets and shops throughout the country.

The Israeli Food Scene: A Fusion of Cultures

Israel's food scene is a fusion of different cultures and culinary traditions. The country's cuisine is influenced by Jewish, Middle Eastern, Mediterranean, and North African cuisine, among others. Israeli food is known for its bold flavors, fresh ingredients, and use of herbs and spices.

One of the unique cultural experiences that Israel has to offer is its food markets. The country is home to many vibrant and bustling markets, such as the Mahane

Yehuda Market in Jerusalem and the Carmel Market in Tel Aviv. These markets offer visitors the opportunity to taste traditional Israeli dishes, such as falafel, hummus, and shakshuka, and to sample local produce and spices.

Israel is also home to many innovative and creative chefs who are pushing the boundaries of traditional cuisine. The country has a thriving restaurant scene, with many high-end restaurants and casual eateries offering a diverse range of culinary experiences.

The Israeli Music Scene: A Fusion of Sounds

Israel's music scene is a fusion of different sounds and musical traditions. The country's music is influenced by Jewish, Middle Eastern, North African, and Western music, among others. Israeli music is known for its diverse range of styles and genres, from traditional folk music to modern pop and rock.

One of the unique cultural experiences that Israel has to offer is its music festivals. The country is home to many music festivals throughout the year, such as the Jerusalem International Oud Festival, the Red Sea Jazz Festival, and the Tamar Festival. These festivals offer visitors the opportunity to experience Israeli music and to enjoy live performances by local and international artists.

Israel is a country that offers a unique cultural experience that is unlike anything else in the world. From the spiritual and cultural center of Jerusalem to the modern and vibrant city of Tel Aviv, from the natural wonder of the Dead Sea to the nomadic way of life of the Bedouin people, from the fusion of flavors in Israeli cuisine to the fusion of sounds in Israeli music, Israel has something to offer everyone. Whether you are interested in history, culture, nature, or simply enjoying good food and music, Israel is a destination that should not be missed.

CHAPTER 10: CULTURE AND ETIQUETTE

Culture and etiquette play an important role in Israeli society. As a country with a diverse population and a complex history, Israel has its own unique customs, traditions, and social norms. Understanding and respecting these cultural nuances is essential for visitors to the country, as it can greatly enhance their travel experience and prevent any cultural misunderstandings.

Religion

Religion plays a significant role in Israeli culture, particularly Judaism, Islam, and Christianity. Israel is considered a holy land by all three religions, and as such, religious customs and traditions are deeply ingrained in daily life. Visitors should be aware of and respectful of religious customs, particularly when visiting holy sites such as the Western Wall or the Dome of the Rock.

In Jewish culture, it is customary for men to wear a kippah, or skullcap, when visiting a synagogue or other religious site. Women should dress modestly, with covered shoulders and knees. It is also customary for men and women to sit separately in some Orthodox synagogues.

In Muslim culture, it is customary to remove shoes when entering a mosque or other religious site. Women should cover their hair and dress modestly, with covered shoulders and knees. It is also important to note that during the month of Ramadan, Muslims fast during daylight hours, so visitors should be respectful of this practice and avoid eating or drinking in public during this time.

In Christian culture, it is customary to dress modestly when visiting holy sites. Visitors should also be respectful of Christian customs, such as taking off hats and sunglasses when entering a church.

Social Customs

Israeli society is known for its warm and friendly hospitality, but there are also certain social customs and norms that visitors should be aware of.

In Israeli culture, it is common to greet people with a kiss on both cheeks, particularly among friends and family. Handshakes are also common, particularly in business settings.

It is important to note that Israelis are known for their direct communication style and can be quite assertive in their interactions. Visitors should not mistake this for rudeness and should try to communicate in a straightforward and direct manner.

Israel is also a society that values punctuality, particularly in business settings. Visitors should make every effort to arrive on time for meetings and appointments.

Dress Code

Israel is a relatively liberal country when it comes to dress, particularly in urban areas such as Tel Aviv. However, visitors should still be mindful of the local dress code, particularly in religious areas or when visiting more conservative communities.

In Jewish and Muslim areas, it is customary for women to dress modestly, with covered shoulders and knees. Men should avoid wearing shorts or sleeveless shirts in these areas.

In more conservative communities, such as ultra-Orthodox Jewish neighborhoods, women should dress modestly, with long skirts and covered shoulders. Men should wear long pants and avoid wearing shorts or sleeveless shirts.

Food and Dining

Israeli cuisine is known for its bold flavors and use of fresh ingredients. Dining out is a popular pastime in Israeli culture, and visitors should be familiar with local dining customs and etiquette.

In Jewish culture, it is customary to bless the food before eating. This is done by reciting the "Hamotzi" prayer before eating bread and the "Shehecheyanu" prayer for special occasions.

In Muslim culture, it is customary to wash hands before eating and to eat with the right hand.

In general, it is considered polite to wait for the host to start eating before beginning to eat. It is also customary to offer to pay for the meal, particularly if you have been invited to dine by a local.

Understanding and respecting Israeli culture and etiquette is essential for visitors to the country. By familiarizing themselves with local customs and norms, visitors can enhance their travel experience and prevent any cultural misunderstandings. Whether visiting holy sites or dining out at a local restaurant, visitors should be mindful of religious customs, dress codes, and social etiquette. By following these guidelines, visitors can show respect for the local culture and enjoy a more authentic travel experience in Israel.

It is also important to note that Israel is a diverse country with a wide range of cultural influences. Visitors may encounter different customs and traditions depending on the region they are visiting or the community they are interacting with. For example, Bedouin culture in the Negev desert has its own unique customs and traditions that differ from those in more urban areas.

Visitors should also be aware of political sensitivities in the country, particularly regarding the Israeli-Palestinian conflict. It is important to avoid discussions of politics or religion in public settings, as these topics can be highly divisive and emotional.

In general, visitors to Israel should approach their interactions with locals in a respectful and open-minded manner. By showing an interest in the local culture and customs, visitors can foster positive relationships with locals and gain a deeper appreciation for the richness and diversity of Israeli society.

Tips for Respectful Behavior and Dress

When traveling to a new country, it is always important to be mindful of cultural differences and respectful of local customs. In Israel, there are certain tips and guidelines that visitors can follow to ensure they are behaving respectfully and dressing appropriately.

1. Dress modestly in religious areas: Israel is a country with a strong religious presence, particularly in areas such as Jerusalem and the Old City. When visiting religious sites, it is

important to dress modestly, with covered shoulders and knees. Women should also cover their hair in certain areas, such as the Western Wall.

2. Respect religious customs: In addition to dressing appropriately, visitors should also be respectful of religious customs and traditions. For example, when visiting a synagogue or mosque, it is customary to remove shoes before entering.

3. Follow local dress codes: While Israel is generally a liberal country when it comes to dress, visitors should still be mindful of local dress codes. In more conservative areas or neighborhoods, such as ultra-Orthodox Jewish communities, women should dress modestly and men should avoid wearing shorts or sleeveless shirts.

4. Show respect for cultural differences: Israel is a diverse country with a wide range of cultural influences. Visitors should approach their interactions

with locals in a respectful and open-minded manner, showing an interest in the local culture and customs.

5. Be mindful of political sensitivities: The Israeli-Palestinian conflict remains a sensitive and emotional topic in the country. Visitors should avoid discussing politics or religion in public settings, as these topics can be highly divisive.

6. Practice good manners: In Israeli culture, it is customary to greet people with a kiss on both cheeks, particularly among friends and family. Handshakes are also common, particularly in business settings. Visitors should also make every effort to arrive on time for meetings and appointments, as punctuality is valued in Israeli society.

By following these tips and guidelines, visitors to Israel can show respect for the local culture and customs, and enjoy a more authentic travel experience.

CHAPTER 11: SAFETY AND SECURITY

Israel is generally a safe and secure country for travelers, but as with any destination, visitors should take precautions to ensure their safety.

Terrorism and Political Tensions

Israel is a country with a complex political history and ongoing conflicts, particularly with neighboring countries and territories. Visitors should be aware of the potential for political tensions and acts of terrorism, particularly in areas near the Gaza Strip and West Bank.

Travelers should stay informed of current events and avoid large gatherings or demonstrations. Visitors should also be aware of their surroundings and report any suspicious activity to the authorities.

Crime

While Israel has a relatively low crime rate, visitors should still take precautions to ensure their safety. Theft and pickpocketing can occur in crowded tourist areas, so travelers should keep valuables secure and be mindful of their surroundings.

Health and Medical Care

Israel has a high standard of healthcare and medical facilities, but visitors should still take precautions to stay healthy while traveling. The country experiences extreme heat during the summer months, so travelers should stay hydrated and avoid prolonged exposure to the sun.

Visitors should also be aware of the risk of food and waterborne illnesses, particularly when consuming street food or drinking tap water. It is recommended to stick to bottled water and avoid uncooked or undercooked food.

Natural Disasters

Israel is not prone to major natural disasters such as hurricanes or earthquakes, but visitors should still be aware of the potential for flash floods and extreme weather conditions.

In the event of an emergency, travelers should follow the instructions of local authorities and seek shelter or evacuate as directed.

Overall, visitors to Israel can enjoy a safe and secure travel experience by staying informed, taking precautions, and using common sense.

Overview of Current Security Situation in Israel

The security situation in Israel is complex and dynamic, with ongoing political tensions and the threat of terrorism. The Israeli-Palestinian conflict, in particular, remains a source of ongoing tension and violence.

In recent years, there have been sporadic outbreaks of violence, including rocket attacks from the Gaza Strip and terrorist attacks in Jerusalem and other parts of the country. The situation is closely monitored by the Israeli government, and visitors are encouraged to stay informed of current events and follow the instructions of local authorities.

In addition to the ongoing conflict, there is also a threat of terrorism from extremist groups such as Hamas, Hezbollah, and ISIS. These groups have targeted Israeli civilians and foreign visitors in the past, and travelers should be aware of the potential for attacks.

The Israeli government has taken steps to enhance security measures in public areas such as airports, transportation hubs, and tourist attractions. Visitors can expect to encounter security checkpoints and screenings when traveling within the country.

While the security situation in Israel can be concerning, it is important to note that the vast majority of visits to the country are safe and without incident. Visitors should take precautions, such as avoiding large gatherings or demonstrations, and be aware of their surroundings.

It is also important to note that the situation can change rapidly, and visitors should stay informed of current events and travel advisories. The US Department of State and other government agencies provide up-to-date travel advisories for Israel and the surrounding region.

Medical and Emergency Services and Resources

Israel has a well-developed healthcare system, with modern facilities and highly trained medical professionals. Visitors to the country can expect to receive high-quality medical care in the event of an emergency.

Emergency Services

In the event of a medical emergency, visitors can call the national emergency number, 101, for assistance. The emergency services in Israel are staffed by trained professionals, including paramedics and emergency physicians.

Ambulance services are available throughout the country, and response times are typically fast. Visitors should be aware that ambulance services are not free, and they may be responsible for the cost of the service, depending on their insurance coverage.

Medical Facilities

Israel has a range of medical facilities, including public and private hospitals, clinics, and emergency care centers. The level of care varies depending on the facility, with some hospitals offering advanced medical treatments and others providing basic care.

Public hospitals in Israel provide high-quality medical care, but they can be crowded and busy, particularly in urban areas. Private hospitals offer a higher level of comfort and personalized care, but they can be more expensive.

Pharmacies and Medications

Pharmacies are widely available in Israel, and visitors can purchase over-the-counter medications without a prescription. However, visitors should be aware that some medications may require a prescription from a local doctor.

In the event that a visitor requires a prescription medication, they can visit a local doctor or hospital to obtain a prescription. It is recommended that visitors bring a copy of their prescription or a list of their medications with them when traveling to Israel.

Travel Insurance

Visitors to Israel are strongly advised to purchase travel insurance that includes medical coverage. This can help cover the cost of medical treatment and emergency services in the event of an illness or injury.

Travel insurance can also provide assistance with arranging medical care and repatriation in the event of a serious medical emergency.

Overall, visitors to Israel can expect to receive high-quality medical care and emergency services in the event of an emergency. However, it is important to take precautions and obtain appropriate travel insurance to ensure that you are fully covered in the event of a medical emergency.

Advice for Staying Safe While Traveling in Israel

Traveling to any foreign country can pose some risks, and Israel is no exception. Here are some tips to help you stay safe while traveling in Israel:

1. Stay informed: Keep up-to-date on the current situation in the country by monitoring local news sources, and following the guidance of local authorities. The US Department of State and other government agencies provide up-to-date travel advisories for Israel and the surrounding region.

2. Be aware of your surroundings: Stay alert and aware of your surroundings at all times. Avoid wandering into unfamiliar areas, particularly at night, and always be aware of your surroundings.

3. Avoid large crowds and demonstrations: Large gatherings, especially those that are political or

religious in nature, can be volatile and potentially dangerous. Avoid these events if possible, and stay away from areas where protests or demonstrations are taking place.

4. Follow security procedures: Expect security checkpoints and screenings when traveling within the country, and comply with the instructions of security personnel.

5. Respect local customs and traditions: Be aware of and respect local customs and traditions. Dress modestly when visiting religious sites, and be mindful of cultural norms when interacting with locals.

6. Use reputable transportation: Use reputable transportation services, such as taxis or licensed tour operators. Be wary of unlicensed taxis or other transportation services, as they may be unsafe.

7. Keep a low profile: Avoid wearing clothing or accessories that identify

you as a tourist, as this can make you a target for criminals or extremists.

8. Secure your valuables: Keep your valuables, such as passports, credit cards, and cash, secure at all times. Consider using a money belt or other hidden storage method to keep these items safe.

9. Use common sense: Use common sense and good judgment when traveling in Israel. If something seems unsafe or uncomfortable, trust your instincts and remove yourself from the situation.

By following these tips, you can help ensure that your trip to Israel is safe and enjoyable. Remember to stay informed, be aware of your surroundings, and use common sense to avoid potential risks.

CHAPTER 12: ISRAEL FOR FAMILIES

Israel is a fantastic destination for families, offering a wealth of cultural, historical, and natural attractions that appeal to all ages. From the bustling cities of Tel Aviv and Jerusalem to the tranquil beaches of the Mediterranean and the Red Sea, there is something for everyone in Israel. Here are some tips for families planning a trip to Israel:

1. Plan ahead: Before you go, do some research on the attractions, activities, and events that are best suited to your family's interests and needs. Consider factors such as age range, mobility, and dietary restrictions when making your plans.

2. Take a guided tour: Consider taking a guided tour of some of the country's most popular attractions. This can be a great way to learn about the history

and culture of the region, while also keeping kids engaged and entertained.

3. Visit the beach: Israel has some beautiful beaches that are perfect for families. Some of the most popular include Tel Aviv Beach, Herzliya Beach, and Eilat Beach. Be sure to bring sunscreen, hats, and plenty of water.

4. Explore the outdoors: Israel has a wealth of natural attractions that are perfect for families, including national parks, nature reserves, and hiking trails. Some of the most popular include Masada National Park, the Ein Gedi Nature Reserve, and the Banias Nature Reserve.

5. Visit family-friendly museums: Israel is home to a number of museums that are ideal for families, including the Israel Museum, the Tel Aviv Museum of Art, and the Bloomfield Science Museum. These museums often have

interactive exhibits and activities that are engaging for kids of all ages.

6. Sample local cuisine: Israeli cuisine is delicious and diverse, with plenty of options for families. Be sure to try some of the local specialties, such as falafel, hummus, and shakshuka.

7. Attend cultural events: Israel has a vibrant cultural scene, with festivals, concerts, and other events taking place throughout the year. Check local listings for events that are suitable for families, such as music festivals, cultural fairs, and children's theater performances.

Overall, Israel offers a wealth of opportunities for families to explore and enjoy together. With careful planning and a sense of adventure, a family trip to Israel can be a truly unforgettable experience.

Family-Friendly Destinations and Attractions

Israel is a fantastic destination for families, with plenty of attractions and activities that cater to all ages. Here are some of the top family-friendly destinations and attractions in Israel:

1. Tel Aviv: Israel's largest city has a youthful, energetic vibe that makes it a great destination for families. Tel Aviv's beaches are some of the best in the country, with soft sand, clear water, and plenty of amenities. Families can also visit the Tel Aviv Port, which is home to restaurants, shops, and a playground.
2. Jerusalem: The ancient city of Jerusalem is a fascinating destination for families, with historical and cultural attractions that will appeal to all ages. The Old City is a UNESCO World Heritage Site and home to numerous religious sites, including the

Western Wall, the Church of the Holy Sepulchre, and the Dome of the Rock. Families can also visit the Israel Museum, which has a children's wing with interactive exhibits.

3. Masada National Park: Masada is an ancient fortress that sits atop a dramatic cliff overlooking the Dead Sea. Families can take a cable car to the top, where they can explore the ruins and take in stunning views of the surrounding desert landscape.

4. Dead Sea: The Dead Sea is a unique natural wonder that is safe and fun for families to enjoy. Kids will love floating in the salty water, which has healing properties for the skin. Families can also visit the nearby Ein Gedi Nature Reserve, which has hiking trails, waterfalls, and pools to swim in.

5. Eilat: Eilat is a resort city on the Red Sea, with beautiful beaches and plenty of activities for families. Kids will love the Coral Beach Nature Reserve,

which has a shallow reef that is perfect for snorkeling. Families can also visit the Underwater Observatory, which offers a glimpse into the colorful marine life of the Red Sea.

6. Haifa: Haifa is a coastal city with a relaxed, family-friendly atmosphere. Families can visit the Bahai Gardens, a stunning series of terraced gardens that are a UNESCO World Heritage Site. The city also has a number of beaches, parks, and museums that are great for families.

7. Timna Park: Timna Park is a desert park that offers a range of activities for families, including hiking, biking, and rock climbing. Kids will love exploring the colorful sandstone formations and ancient copper mines.

Overall, Israel offers plenty of family-friendly destinations and attractions that will appeal to all ages. With careful planning and a sense of adventure, a family trip to Israel can be a truly unforgettable experience.

Kid-Friendly Attractions and Activities

Israel is a great destination for families with kids, as there are plenty of attractions and activities that cater to children of all ages. From zoos and aquariums to museums and science centers, Israel offers a variety of opportunities for kids to learn, explore, and have fun. Here are some of the top kid-friendly attractions and activities in Israel:

1. Zoos and Aquariums

Israel has several zoos and aquariums that are perfect for kids. These attractions offer a unique opportunity for kids to see and learn about animals from all over the world. Here are some of the top zoos and aquariums in Israel:

- Jerusalem Biblical Zoo: This popular destination features animals from the Bible and offers a variety of interactive exhibits. Kids can see lions, tigers, giraffes, zebras, and other animals up close and learn about their habitats and behaviors. The zoo also offers a petting zoo, playground, and train ride.
- Eilat Underwater Observatory Marine Park: This marine park is a hit with kids, as it features a range of marine life and offers opportunities for kids to touch and feed some of the animals. Kids can see sharks, rays, sea turtles, and other fish through the underwater observatory, or take a glass-bottom boat tour to see them in their natural habitat.
- Hai-Kef Zoo: This small zoo in Haifa is perfect for younger children, as it features a range of domestic animals and birds. Kids can pet rabbits, guinea

pigs, and other animals, or watch parrots and other birds perform tricks.

2. Museums and Science Centers

Israel has several museums and science centers that are great for kids. These attractions offer hands-on exhibits and interactive activities that encourage learning and exploration. Here are some of the top museums and science centers in Israel:

- Bloomfield Science Museum: This museum in Jerusalem is a popular destination, as it offers interactive exhibits on science and technology. Kids can learn about space, electricity, sound, and other scientific concepts through hands-on activities and experiments.
- Israel Children's Museum: This museum in Holon is a hit with kids, as it features exhibits and activities that encourage learning and exploration. Kids can play in a giant ball pit, build

with blocks, or climb through a maze of tunnels.

- Madatech: This science museum in Haifa offers a range of exhibits on physics, chemistry, and other scientific topics. Kids can play with magnets, build structures with blocks, or try their hand at engineering challenges.

3. Parks and Playgrounds

Israel has many parks and playgrounds that are perfect for kids to run around and play. These attractions offer a chance for kids to enjoy the great outdoors and get some exercise. Here are some of the top parks and playgrounds in Israel:

- Yarkon Park: This park in Tel Aviv is a popular destination, as it offers playgrounds, bike trails, and boat rentals. Kids can play on swings, slides, and climbing structures, or rent a boat and paddle around the lake.

- Ein Gedi Nature Reserve: This nature reserve in the Dead Sea region is a hit with kids, as it features waterfalls and pools to swim in. Kids can splash around in the water and explore the natural surroundings.
- Ariel Sharon Park: This park in Tel Aviv is built on top of a former landfill and offers a range of activities for kids. Kids can climb on a giant slide, ride a zip line, or play in the sandbox.

4. Beaches

Israel has some of the best beaches in the world, and they are great for kids to enjoy. These attractions offer a chance for kids to swim, play in the sand, and soak up the sun. Here are some of the top beaches in Israel:

- Tel Aviv Beaches: The beaches in Tel Aviv are a popular destination for families with kids, as they offer soft sand, clear water, and a range of activities. Kids can swim in the water, play in the sand, or try their hand at beach volleyball.

- Eilat Beaches: The beaches in Eilat are perfect for kids, as they offer calm water and a range of water activities. Kids can snorkel, swim with dolphins, or ride a banana boat.
- Haifa Beaches: The beaches in Haifa offer a unique experience, as they are nestled at the foot of the Carmel Mountains. Kids can enjoy the clear water and soft sand, or take a hike up the mountain for some stunning views.

5.   Amusement Parks

Israel has several amusement parks that are perfect for families with kids. These attractions offer a range of rides and activities that are sure to thrill kids of all ages. Here are some of the top amusement parks in Israel:

- Luna Park: This amusement park in Tel Aviv offers a range of rides and attractions for kids, including roller coasters, bumper cars, and a Ferris wheel. There are also games and snacks available for purchase.
- Superland: This amusement park in Rishon LeZion is a hit with kids, as it features a range of rides and attractions for all ages. Kids can ride roller coasters, bumper cars, and a giant swing, or play mini-golf and other games.
- Adventure Park: This amusement park in Kfar Saba offers a range of outdoor activities, including zip-lining, rock climbing, and rope courses. There are also trampolines and a giant slide for kids to enjoy.

Overall, Israel is a great destination for families with kids, as there are plenty of attractions and activities to keep everyone entertained. Whether you're looking for museums, zoos, beaches, or amusement parks, Israel has something for everyone. Just be sure to plan ahead and take the necessary precautions to ensure a safe and enjoyable trip.

Tips for Traveling with Children

Traveling with children can be both exciting and challenging. Whether you are traveling with infants, toddlers, or older children, there are a few tips that can make the experience smoother and more enjoyable for everyone. Here are some tips for traveling with children:

1. Pack Wisely: Make a list of essential items you will need for your children and pack accordingly. Be sure to include plenty of diapers, wipes, clothes, and any necessary medications. You can also pack some new toys or games to keep your children entertained during the journey.

2. Be Flexible: Traveling with children can be unpredictable, so be prepared to be flexible with your schedule and plans. Allow extra time for unexpected stops or delays, and be ready to change plans if necessary.

3. Choose Child-Friendly Accommodations: Look for hotels or accommodations that cater to families with children. Consider factors like proximity to attractions, safety, and amenities such as pools, playgrounds, or kids' clubs.

4. Plan for Naps and Rest Time: Young children need plenty of rest and naps, so plan for regular breaks during the day. This will help prevent meltdowns and tantrums, and ensure that everyone has enough energy to enjoy the trip.

5. Bring Snacks: Children can get hungry easily, so be sure to pack plenty of snacks and drinks. This will help keep them nourished and hydrated

throughout the trip, and also save money on food expenses.

6. Keep Your Children Safe: Be sure to take necessary safety precautions, such as using car seats, keeping a close eye on your children in crowded areas, and teaching them about the local customs and culture.

7. Involve Your Children in the Planning Process: Get your children involved in the planning process by asking for their input on activities and destinations. This will help them feel more engaged and excited about the trip.

8. Stay Calm: Children can sense when their parents are stressed or anxious, so try to stay calm and positive throughout the journey. This will help create a more relaxed and enjoyable atmosphere for everyone.

By following these tips, you can help make your family trip a success and create lasting memories for you and your children.

Childcare Options and Resources

If you are traveling to Israel with children, there are several childcare options and resources available to help you make the most of your trip. Here are some options to consider:

1. Hotel Babysitting Services: Many hotels in Israel offer babysitting services for their guests. These services are usually provided by trained professionals who have been background-checked and are experienced with working with children. Check with your hotel to see if they offer this service and what the rates are.

2. Childcare Referral Services: In Israel, there are several websites and agencies that provide childcare referral services. These services can help connect you with qualified

babysitters, nannies, or daycare providers in the area you are visiting. Some popular referral services in Israel include Mamanet, Hamavrik, and Tel Aviv Babysitters.

3. Local Parenting Groups: Joining a local parenting group can be a great way to connect with other parents and find childcare recommendations. These groups can be found through social media or community bulletin boards. Some popular parenting groups in Israel include Beit Hakerem Moms in Jerusalem and Haifa Parents Club in Haifa.

4. Online Caregiver Platforms: There are several online caregiver platforms such as Care.com, Sittercity, and UrbanSitter that connect families with qualified babysitters and nannies. These platforms typically require background checks and allow parents to read reviews from other families who have used their services.

5. Drop-in Childcare Centers: Some cities in Israel, such as Tel Aviv, have drop-in childcare centers that allow parents to leave their children for a few hours while they run errands or attend appointments. These centers usually require reservations and charge by the hour.
6. Family-Friendly Attractions: Many family-friendly attractions in Israel, such as zoos and amusement parks, offer childcare services or supervised play areas. This can be a great option if you want to enjoy some adult time while your children are entertained.

When choosing a childcare option, it is important to research and vet the provider or service to ensure that your children will be in safe and capable hands. You may also want to ask for recommendations from other parents or local expat groups to help you find the best option for your family.

CHAPTER 13: ISRAEL FOR ADVENTURE-SEEKERS

If you're an adventure-seeker, Israel has plenty of activities to offer. From exploring natural wonders to experiencing adrenaline-pumping activities, here are some top adventure activities to consider during your trip to Israel:

1. Hiking: Israel is a hiker's paradise, with numerous trails that range from easy to challenging. The Israel National Trail is a 620-mile trek that stretches from the northern border to the southern tip of Israel, passing through mountains, deserts, and forests. For those looking for a shorter hike, there are plenty of day hikes to choose from, such as the Ein Gedi Nature Reserve, the Masada Sunrise Hike, and the Banias Waterfall Trail.

2. Scuba Diving: Israel's Red Sea coast is a popular destination for scuba divers. With clear waters, vibrant coral reefs,

and diverse marine life, it offers some of the best diving in the world. Eilat, in particular, is a popular diving destination, with several dive centers offering beginner and advanced courses, as well as guided dives.

3. Rock Climbing: Israel's diverse landscapes provide plenty of opportunities for rock climbing. The Ramon Crater, located in the Negev Desert, is a popular spot for climbers of all levels. The area offers a range of climbing routes, from beginner to advanced, with stunning desert views as a backdrop.

4. Hot Air Balloon Rides: Hot air balloon rides offer a unique way to experience Israel's stunning landscapes from above. The Jezreel Valley and the Galilee are popular spots for hot air balloon rides, offering panoramic views of the surrounding mountains and valleys.

5. Surfing: Israel's Mediterranean coast is a popular spot for surfing, with waves that are suitable for both beginners and experienced surfers. Surf schools and rental shops can be found in popular beach towns such as Tel Aviv, Netanya, and Haifa.
6. Skydiving: For thrill-seekers, skydiving is an unforgettable experience. Skydive Israel offers tandem skydiving over the Mediterranean Sea, with stunning views of the coastline and the city of Tel Aviv.
7. ATV Tours: ATV tours offer a fun and adventurous way to explore Israel's deserts and mountains. Several companies offer guided ATV tours, including the Negev Desert, the Golan Heights, and the Galilee.

When planning adventure activities in Israel, it's important to take safety precautions and choose reputable companies or guides. Make sure to research the activity and provider beforehand, and always follow safety instructions and guidelines. With the right planning and precautions, Israel can offer a thrilling and unforgettable adventure experience.

National Parks and Nature Reserves

Israel is a country with a rich and diverse landscape, ranging from mountains to deserts to coastlines. This makes it an ideal destination for nature lovers and adventure-seekers alike. Here are some of the top national parks and nature reserves to explore during your visit:

1. Masada National Park: Located in the Judean Desert, Masada National Park is home to the ancient fortress of Masada, a UNESCO World Heritage site. Visitors can hike up to the fortress to enjoy panoramic views of the desert landscape, or take a cable car to the top. The park also features a visitor center with exhibits and

audio-visual presentations about the history of Masada.

2. Ein Gedi Nature Reserve: This nature reserve is located near the Dead Sea and is home to a variety of plant and animal species, including ibex, hyraxes, and birds of prey. Visitors can hike through the reserve to enjoy the waterfalls, natural pools, and hot springs. The reserve also features a botanical garden with over 900 plant species.

3. Timna Park: Located in the southern Negev Desert, Timna Park is home to unique geological formations, including the famous "Mushroom" rock. Visitors can also explore ancient copper mines, dating back to the Bronze Age, and enjoy hiking trails and mountain biking routes.

4. Banias Nature Reserve: Located in the Golan Heights, Banias Nature Reserve is home to the Banias waterfall, the largest waterfall in Israel. Visitors can

also explore the ancient city of Caesarea Philippi, dating back to the Roman period, and hike through the reserve to enjoy the natural scenery.

5. Carmel Hai-Bar Nature Reserve: This nature reserve, located in the Carmel Mountains, is home to a variety of endangered species, including the Persian fallow deer, the Mediterranean wildcat, and the Griffon vulture. Visitors can take a guided tour of the reserve to learn about the conservation efforts and see the animals up close.

6. Yarkon Park: Located in the heart of Tel Aviv, Yarkon Park is a popular destination for locals and visitors alike. The park features botanical gardens, a lake, bike trails, and picnic areas. It also hosts concerts and events throughout the year.

When visiting these parks and reserves, it is important to follow the guidelines and regulations to ensure the preservation of the natural environment. This includes not littering, staying on designated trails, and respecting wildlife and plant life.

CHAPTER 14: TRAVELING WITH DISABILITIES

Traveling with a disability can present unique challenges, but with careful planning and preparation, it is possible to have an enjoyable and fulfilling travel experience. Here are some tips and resources for traveling with disabilities in Israel:

1. Plan ahead: Before you travel, research your destination and any accommodations or accessibility features that may be available. This may include wheelchair ramps, accessible public transportation, and wheelchair-friendly accommodations. It is also a good idea to research the local laws and customs related to disabilities to avoid any misunderstandings or cultural barriers.

2. Consider transportation: When traveling with a disability, transportation can be a major

concern. In Israel, public transportation is generally accessible and accommodating to travelers with disabilities. Buses and trains have designated seating and ramps for wheelchair users, and taxis are required by law to provide service to passengers with disabilities. You may also consider renting a car with hand controls or other accessibility features.

3. Choose accessible accommodations: When booking accommodations, look for hotels or rental properties that are wheelchair accessible or have other accommodations for travelers with disabilities. Many hotels and vacation rentals now offer accessible rooms with features such as roll-in showers, grab bars, and lower countertops. You may also consider staying in an apartment or villa with a kitchen to allow for greater independence and flexibility during your stay.

4. Know your rights: In Israel, there are laws and regulations in place to protect the rights of people with disabilities. These include accessibility requirements for public buildings and transportation, as well as anti-discrimination laws in the workplace and other areas. If you encounter any issues or barriers during your travels, it is important to

know your rights and advocate for yourself.

5. Use accessible tours and guides: Many tour companies and guides in Israel offer accessible tours and excursions for travelers with disabilities. These may include wheelchair-accessible tours of historical sites or outdoor activities adapted for people with mobility impairments. Working with a tour operator who is familiar with your specific needs and requirements can make your trip more enjoyable and stress-free.

6. Accessible resources: There are several resources available for travelers with disabilities in Israel. The Israel Society for the Deaf provides information and resources for travelers with hearing impairments, while Access Israel is a nonprofit organization dedicated to promoting accessibility and inclusion for people with disabilities. The Israel Ministry of Tourism also provides

information and resources for travelers with disabilities, including a guide to accessible tourism in Israel.

7. Consider travel insurance: Travel insurance can provide peace of mind in case of unexpected emergencies or medical needs during your trip. When selecting travel insurance, be sure to check the coverage for pre-existing conditions and any specific needs related to your disability.

Overall, traveling with a disability in Israel may present some challenges, but with careful planning and preparation, it is possible to have a safe and enjoyable travel experience. By researching your destination, choosing accessible accommodations and transportation, and working with experienced tour operators and guides, you can create a memorable and fulfilling trip to Israel.

Accessibility Resources and Accommodations

Israel has made strides in improving accessibility for people with disabilities in recent years, but there is still progress to be made. Here are some resources and accommodations available for travelers with disabilities in Israel:

1. Accessibility in public transportation: The majority of public transportation in Israel is accessible to people with disabilities. Buses and trains have designated seating and ramps for wheelchair users, and many stations and bus stops have been upgraded to include accessible features such as tactile paving and audio announcements. The Israel Railways website provides information on accessible services and stations.

2. Accessible accommodations: Many hotels and vacation rentals in Israel offer accessible rooms and

accommodations for travelers with disabilities. These may include roll-in showers, grab bars, and lowered countertops. The Israel Ministry of Tourism provides a list of accessible accommodations on their website.

3. Accessible attractions and tours: Many historical sites, museums, and attractions in Israel have made efforts to improve accessibility for visitors with disabilities. Some offer audio or visual guides, wheelchair ramps, and accessible seating. There are also tour companies and guides that specialize in accessible tours for people with disabilities.

4. Service animals: Service animals are allowed in public places and transportation in Israel. However, it is recommended to carry documentation proving that the animal is a trained service animal.

5. Accessibility resources: There are several organizations in Israel

dedicated to promoting accessibility for people with disabilities. Access Israel is a nonprofit organization that works to improve accessibility and inclusion in all areas of society. The Israel Society for the Deaf provides resources and information for travelers with hearing impairments.

6. Disability parking permits: People with disabilities can apply for a disability parking permit in Israel, which allows them to park in designated disabled parking spaces. The permit is recognized throughout Israel and is valid for a period of five years.

7. Wheelchair rentals: Many tourist attractions and sites offer wheelchair rentals, including the Israel Museum and Yad Vashem Holocaust Museum.

It is important to note that accessibility varies greatly depending on the location and attraction, and not all areas of Israel may be fully accessible. It is recommended to do research and contact the venue or attraction beforehand to inquire about accessibility features and accommodations.

Barrier-Free Travel Tips

Traveling with a disability can present unique challenges, but with proper planning and research, it is possible to have a barrier-free travel experience in Israel. Here are some tips for traveling with a disability:

1. Research accessibility: Before booking your trip, research the accessibility of your destination and the places you plan to visit. Check websites and contact the venues or attractions to inquire about accessibility features and accommodations. It is also helpful to read reviews from other travelers with disabilities to get an idea of their experiences.
2. Plan your transportation: Research accessible transportation options in advance, such as accessible taxis or

rental cars with hand controls. If you plan to use public transportation, check the accessibility features of the bus or train lines you will be using. It is also recommended to have a backup plan in case the transportation you planned to use is not accessible.

3. Pack necessary equipment: Bring any necessary equipment or mobility aids, such as a wheelchair, crutches, or a walker. It is also a good idea to bring extra batteries, chargers, or adaptors for your equipment.

4. Consider accommodations: When booking accommodations, look for accessible rooms or vacation rentals that meet your needs. Ask about roll-in showers, grab bars, and other accessibility features. It is also helpful to request a room on a lower floor or near an elevator for easier access.

5. Inform your airline: If you are flying, inform your airline of your disability and any special accommodations you

may need. Airlines are required to provide assistance with boarding and deplaning, and can also provide assistance with baggage.

6. Consider travel insurance: It is a good idea to purchase travel insurance that covers medical emergencies and trip cancellation, especially if you have a pre-existing medical condition.

7. Bring medication and medical records: Bring any necessary medication and a copy of your medical records with you. It is also recommended to bring a letter from your doctor outlining your medical condition and any special accommodations you may need.

8. Know your rights: Familiarize yourself with your rights as a traveler with a disability, including the Americans with Disabilities Act (ADA) and the Air Carrier Access Act (ACAA). These laws protect your rights to accessible transportation and accommodations.

By taking these steps and doing proper research and planning, you can have a barrier-free travel experience in Israel. Remember to also be flexible and patient, as unexpected challenges may arise.

Disability-Friendly Destinations and Activities

Israel has made significant strides in recent years to become more accessible to travelers with disabilities. Here are some of the top disability-friendly destinations and activities in Israel:

1. Old City of Jerusalem: The Old City of Jerusalem has made significant improvements to become more accessible to travelers with disabilities, including the installation of wheelchair ramps and elevators in many of the historic sites and attractions. The Western Wall also offers a special section for disabled visitors.

2. Tel Aviv Beaches: The beaches of Tel Aviv offer accessibility mats and wheelchairs for visitors with mobility impairments, as well as accessible shower and changing facilities.
3. The Dead Sea: The Dead Sea offers a unique experience for travelers with disabilities, with several beaches and resorts offering accessible facilities and activities, such as wheelchair-accessible trails and floating wheelchair rentals.
4. Ramat Gan Safari Park: The Ramat Gan Safari Park offers accessible safari tours and animal encounters, as well as wheelchair-accessible paths throughout the park.
5. Yad Vashem Holocaust Museum: Yad Vashem offers accessibility features such as wheelchair ramps, elevators, and accessible restrooms throughout the museum, as well as guided tours for visitors with hearing or visual impairments.

6. Masada National Park: Masada National Park offers accessible paths and facilities for visitors with disabilities, as well as a wheelchair-accessible cable car to reach the top of the mountain.

7. Haifa's Bahai Gardens: The Bahai Gardens in Haifa offer wheelchair-accessible paths and tours, as well as a shuttle service for visitors with mobility impairments.

8. Caesarea National Park: Caesarea National Park offers accessible paths and facilities for visitors with disabilities, as well as guided tours for visitors with hearing or visual impairments.

9. Accessible hiking trails: Israel has several accessible hiking trails, including the Haifa Trail, the Herzliya Shoreline Trail, and the Sea of Galilee Trail, which offer wheelchair-accessible paths and facilities.

10. Accessible museums and cultural sites: Many of Israel's museums and cultural sites, such as the Israel Museum and the Tel Aviv Museum of Art, offer accessibility features such as wheelchair ramps, elevators, and accessible restrooms.

These destinations and activities are just a few examples of the many disability-friendly options available in Israel. With proper research and planning, travelers with disabilities can have a fulfilling and enjoyable trip to Israel.

CHAPTER 15: LGBTQ+ TRAVEL IN ISRAEL

Israel has become known as a LGBTQ+ friendly destination in recent years, with a vibrant and visible LGBTQ+ community and a growing number of LGBTQ+ friendly businesses, events, and attractions. Here are some tips and recommendations for LGBTQ+ travelers visiting Israel:

1. Tel Aviv Pride: Tel Aviv is known as the LGBTQ+ capital of the Middle East and hosts one of the largest Pride festivals in the world. Tel Aviv Pride takes place in June and includes a parade, parties, concerts, and cultural events.

2. LGBTQ+ friendly businesses: Many businesses in Israel are openly LGBTQ+ friendly, including hotels, restaurants, bars, and clubs. Look for businesses that display the "Pride Flag" or "Rainbow Flag" stickers in

their windows, which indicate their support for the LGBTQ+ community.

3. Gay-friendly neighborhoods: Tel Aviv's Florentin and Rothschild Boulevard neighborhoods are known for their LGBTQ+ friendly atmosphere, with many gay bars, clubs, and restaurants located in these areas.

4. LGBTQ+ cultural events: Israel hosts several LGBTQ+ cultural events throughout the year, including film festivals, theater productions, and art exhibits.

5. LGBTQ+ tours: Several tour companies offer LGBTQ+ specific tours of Israel, which include visits to LGBTQ+ cultural sites, events, and businesses.

6. Legal protections: Israel has legal protections for LGBTQ+ individuals, including anti-discrimination laws and recognition of same-sex marriages performed abroad.

7. Jerusalem Open House: The Jerusalem Open House is an LGBTQ+ community center located in Jerusalem, which offers support services, cultural events, and a safe space for LGBTQ+ individuals in the city.
8. LGBTQ+ organizations: Israel has several LGBTQ+ organizations that offer support, advocacy, and resources for LGBTQ+ individuals, including the Aguda and the Jerusalem Open House.

While Israel has made significant progress in becoming a LGBTQ+ friendly destination, it is important to note that there are still pockets of discrimination and intolerance in some parts of the country. It is always important to exercise caution and respect local customs and laws while traveling, and to be aware of the risks and challenges that may be unique to LGBTQ+ travelers in Israel.

LGBTQ+ Friendly Destinations and Activities

Israel offers many LGBTQ+ friendly destinations and activities for travelers. Here are some recommendations:

1. Tel Aviv: Tel Aviv is the most LGBTQ+ friendly city in Israel, with a vibrant gay scene, including gay bars, clubs, and restaurants. Tel Aviv Pride is a must-visit event for LGBTQ+ travelers, attracting visitors from all over the world.
2. Jerusalem: Jerusalem has a growing LGBTQ+ scene, with several gay bars, clubs, and events, and the Jerusalem Open House, which offers support services and a safe space for LGBTQ+ individuals.
3. Haifa: Haifa is another city in Israel with a growing LGBTQ+ scene, with several gay bars and clubs.

4. Eilat: Eilat is a popular vacation spot for LGBTQ+ travelers, with several LGBTQ+ friendly hotels and a growing gay scene.
5. LGBTQ+ tours: Several tour companies offer LGBTQ+ specific tours of Israel, which include visits to LGBTQ+ cultural sites, events, and businesses.
6. Beaches: Israel has several LGBTQ+ friendly beaches, including Hilton Beach in Tel Aviv and Ga'ash Beach north of Tel Aviv.
7. Museums and cultural events: Many of Israel's museums and cultural events are LGBTQ+ friendly, including the Tel Aviv Museum of Art and the Tel Aviv International LGBT Film Festival.
8. LGBTQ+ organizations: Israel has several LGBTQ+ organizations that offer support, advocacy, and resources for LGBTQ+ individuals, including the

Aguda and the Jerusalem Open House.

Overall, Israel offers many LGBTQ+ friendly destinations and activities for travelers, and continues to make progress in becoming a more inclusive and welcoming destination for the LGBTQ+ community.

LGBTQ+ Rights and Culture in Israel

LGBTQ+ rights and culture in Israel have come a long way in recent years, although challenges still exist. Here is an overview of LGBTQ+ rights and culture in Israel:

Legal Status: Homosexuality was decriminalized in Israel in 1988. In 1992, Israel passed a law prohibiting discrimination based on sexual orientation, making it one of the first countries in the world to do so. Same-sex couples are recognized for inheritance purposes and are able to adopt children. Additionally, in 2020, Israel passed a law allowing same-sex couples to use surrogacy.

Gay Marriage: While same-sex marriage is not yet recognized in Israel, same-sex couples who marry abroad are recognized as married in Israel. In 2019, the Israeli government approved a bill that would allow same-sex couples to adopt children in Israel, although the bill has not yet been fully implemented.

Public Attitudes: Public attitudes towards LGBTQ+ individuals in Israel vary. While Tel Aviv is known for being a very LGBTQ+ friendly city, other parts of Israel may be less accepting. The majority of Israelis are supportive of LGBTQ+ rights, but there are still some who hold negative attitudes towards the community.

LGBTQ+ Organizations: Israel has several LGBTQ+ organizations that provide support and advocacy for LGBTQ+ individuals, including the Aguda and the Jerusalem Open House.

LGBTQ+ Events: There are several LGBTQ+ events held throughout Israel each year. Tel Aviv Pride is the largest event, attracting thousands of visitors from around the world. Other events include the Jerusalem Pride Parade and the Haifa Pride Parade.

LGBTQ+ Culture: The LGBTQ+ community in Israel is diverse and vibrant, with a growing number of LGBTQ+ cultural events, organizations, and businesses. There are several LGBTQ+ bars, clubs, and restaurants in Tel Aviv, as well as LGBTQ+ friendly beaches and hotels.

Overall, Israel has made significant strides in LGBTQ+ rights and culture in recent years, although challenges still exist. The LGBTQ+ community in Israel continues to fight for full equality and acceptance.

Resources for LGBTQ+ Travelers

For LGBTQ+ travelers, there are several resources available in Israel:

1. Aguda - The National Association of LGBTQ+ in Israel: Aguda is the largest and oldest LGBTQ+ organization in Israel, providing a wide range of support services, advocacy, and community outreach programs for LGBTQ+ individuals.
2. Jerusalem Open House: The Jerusalem Open House is an LGBTQ+ community center located in Jerusalem, offering a range of social and support services, including counseling, youth groups, and cultural events.
3. Tel Aviv Gay Vibe: Tel Aviv Gay Vibe is a comprehensive online guide to the LGBTQ+ scene in Tel Aviv, offering information on bars, clubs, events, and hotels.

4. Gaycities: Gaycities is a travel website that offers LGBTQ+ travelers a guide to LGBTQ+ friendly destinations around the world, including Israel.

5. IGLTA - International Gay and Lesbian Travel Association: The IGLTA is a global organization dedicated to LGBTQ+ tourism, offering resources, networking, and advocacy for LGBTQ+ travelers.

6. LGBTQ+ Friendly Accommodations: Many hotels and accommodations in Israel are LGBTQ+ friendly, and some specifically cater to the LGBTQ+ community, including the Brown Hotels, which have several locations in Tel Aviv.

7. LGBTQ+ Events: There are several LGBTQ+ events held throughout Israel each year, including Tel Aviv Pride, Jerusalem Pride, and Haifa Pride, as well as other cultural and social events organized by LGBTQ+ organizations.

Overall, LGBTQ+ travelers can find a range of resources and support in Israel, with many organizations and businesses working to create a welcoming and inclusive environment for all travelers.

CHAPTER 16: VOLUNTEER AND SERVICE OPPORTUNITIES

There are a variety of volunteer and service opportunities available for travelers visiting Israel. These opportunities can provide a unique and meaningful way to experience the culture and give back to the local community.

1. WWOOF Israel: WWOOF stands for Worldwide Opportunities on Organic Farms. This program connects volunteers with organic farmers in Israel, where they can work and learn about sustainable agriculture practices.

2. Israel Volunteer Association: The Israel Volunteer Association is a nonprofit organization that connects volunteers with a variety of service opportunities throughout Israel, including working with children, the elderly, and people with disabilities.

3. Save a Child's Heart: Save a Child's Heart is an Israeli nonprofit organization that provides life-saving heart surgeries for children from developing countries. Volunteers can assist with fundraising, events, and outreach efforts.

4. Leket Israel: Leket Israel is the largest food bank in Israel, providing food assistance to those in need. Volunteers can help with harvesting, sorting, and distributing food to those in need.

5. Green Course: Green Course is an Israeli nonprofit organization that focuses on environmental issues and sustainable development. Volunteers can assist with a variety of projects, including beach cleanups, educational programs, and tree-planting initiatives.

6. Yad Sarah: Yad Sarah is a nonprofit organization that provides medical and rehabilitative equipment for people with disabilities and the

elderly. Volunteers can assist with a variety of tasks, including equipment maintenance, delivery, and outreach efforts.

7. The Abraham Hostel: The Abraham Hostel is a social hostel in Jerusalem that offers a variety of volunteer opportunities, including helping with cultural events, social initiatives, and community outreach efforts.

These are just a few examples of the many volunteer and service opportunities available in Israel. Whether you are interested in environmental conservation, social justice, or education, there are numerous organizations and programs that can provide a meaningful and fulfilling experience for travelers looking to give back to the local community.

Volunteer Organizations and Opportunities

There are many volunteer organizations and opportunities available for travelers who wish to give back and make a positive impact while visiting Israel. Here are a few examples:

1. Masa Israel Journey: Masa Israel Journey is a program that provides a variety of volunteer opportunities, internships, and other experiences in Israel for young adults. Participants can work in areas such as social justice, education, and environmental conservation, among others.

2. Tevel b'Tzedek: Tevel b'Tzedek is a nonprofit organization that works to promote sustainable development and social justice in Israel and other countries. Volunteers can assist with a variety of projects, such as community organizing, agriculture, and education.

3. Amirim: Amirim is a nonprofit organization that focuses on empowering marginalized communities in Israel. Volunteers can assist with projects such as refugee assistance, education, and social justice initiatives.

4. HaTikva Project: HaTikva Project is a nonprofit organization that provides educational and social support for at-risk youth in Israel. Volunteers can assist with mentoring, tutoring, and other educational and social initiatives.
5. Budo for Peace: Budo for Peace is a nonprofit organization that uses martial arts as a tool to promote peace, understanding, and cultural exchange in Israel and other countries. Volunteers can assist with organizing events, fundraising, and outreach efforts.
6. Sadaka-Reut: Sadaka-Reut is a nonprofit organization that works to promote social justice and equality in Israel. Volunteers can assist with a variety of projects, such as community organizing, advocacy, and education.
7. Shalom Corps: Shalom Corps is a program that provides volunteer opportunities in Israel for Jewish

young adults from around the world. Participants can work in areas such as education, community development, and environmental conservation.

These are just a few examples of the many volunteer organizations and opportunities available in Israel. Whether you are interested in education, social justice, environmental conservation, or another area of focus, there are many ways to make a positive impact while experiencing the culture and beauty of Israel.

Sustainable and Responsible Tourism Initiatives

Sustainable and responsible tourism initiatives have become increasingly important in recent years, as travelers become more aware of their impact on the environment and local communities. Israel has a number of initiatives aimed at promoting sustainable and responsible tourism, including the following:

1. Eco-Tourism in the Galilee: The Galilee region of northern Israel offers a variety of eco-tourism experiences, such as hiking and biking trails, bird watching, and organic farming tours. These experiences are designed to promote sustainable tourism while providing visitors with a unique and authentic glimpse of Israel's natural beauty.

2. Green Pilgrimage: The Green Pilgrimage initiative is aimed at promoting sustainable tourism for religious visitors to Israel. The initiative includes a variety of programs and activities designed to raise awareness of environmental issues and promote sustainable travel practices among religious visitors.

3. Sustainable Hospitality: A number of hotels and hospitality companies in Israel have adopted sustainable practices, such as reducing energy and water consumption, using local and

organic food, and recycling waste. Some examples include the Inbal Jerusalem Hotel, which has implemented a variety of sustainable practices such as solar energy and water conservation measures, and the Alegra Boutique Hotel in Tel Aviv, which is committed to reducing its carbon footprint through a variety of initiatives.

4. Community-Based Tourism: Community-based tourism initiatives are designed to promote sustainable tourism while supporting local communities. These initiatives include home-stays and tours run by local residents, as well as initiatives aimed at promoting sustainable livelihoods for local communities.

5. The Dead Sea Preservation Campaign: The Dead Sea, located in the Jordan Valley, is a unique natural wonder that is rapidly disappearing due to human activity. The Dead Sea Preservation

Campaign is a joint initiative between Israel, Jordan, and the Palestinian Authority aimed at promoting sustainable tourism while raising awareness of the importance of preserving the Dead Sea for future generations.

6. Responsible Adventure Travel: A number of adventure travel companies in Israel offer responsible and sustainable travel options, such as low-impact hiking and biking tours and eco-friendly camping experiences.

7. Sustainable Cultural Tourism: Israel is home to a rich and diverse cultural heritage, including historic sites, museums, and traditional crafts. Sustainable cultural tourism initiatives aim to promote responsible tourism practices while supporting the preservation of Israel's cultural heritage.

These are just a few examples of the many sustainable and responsible tourism initiatives taking place in Israel. By supporting these initiatives, travelers can make a positive impact on the environment and local communities while enjoying all that Israel has to offer.

CHAPTER 17: SHOPPING IN ISRAEL

Israel offers a unique shopping experience, blending modern and traditional styles with Middle Eastern influences. From open-air markets to high-end boutiques, there are a variety of shopping options for visitors to explore.

Here are some popular shopping destinations and tips for shopping in Israel:

1. Carmel Market: Located in Tel Aviv, Carmel Market is a bustling open-air

market offering everything from fresh produce to clothing and souvenirs. The market is a great place to find unique items and experience the lively atmosphere of the city.

2. Mahane Yehuda Market: Located in Jerusalem, Mahane Yehuda Market is a colorful and vibrant market offering a wide variety of food, spices, clothing, and souvenirs. The market is particularly lively on Fridays, when locals come to shop for the Sabbath.

3. Old Jaffa: The historic neighborhood of Old Jaffa, located in Tel Aviv, offers a unique shopping experience with its winding streets and alleyways filled with small shops and boutiques. Visitors can find handmade crafts, jewelry, and clothing, as well as local art galleries and antique shops.

4. Designer Boutiques: For those looking for high-end designer clothing and accessories, Tel Aviv and Jerusalem both offer a selection of luxury

boutiques featuring local and international designers.

5. Souvenirs: Israel is known for its unique handicrafts, such as olive wood carvings, ceramics, and jewelry. Visitors can find these items in markets and shops throughout the country.

Tips for Shopping in Israel:

1. Bargaining: Bargaining is common in markets and smaller shops in Israel, but is generally not practiced in larger stores and boutiques. It is important

to be polite and respectful when bargaining.

2. Cash or Credit: While credit cards are widely accepted in Israel, it is still a good idea to carry cash for smaller purchases and in markets.

3. Value Added Tax (VAT): Visitors can claim a VAT refund on purchases over 400 shekels at participating stores by presenting their passport and a completed tax-free form at the airport.

4. Shopping Hours: Most stores in Israel are closed on Saturdays for the Sabbath, but are open during the rest of the week. However, some smaller shops and markets may close early on Fridays.

5. Shipping: Many shops offer shipping services for larger items and souvenirs, which can be a convenient option for travelers.

Shopping in Israel offers visitors a unique opportunity to explore local markets and boutiques while discovering the country's vibrant culture and history. With a little preparation and some bargaining skills, visitors can find a variety of unique and memorable items to bring back home.

Traditional Souks and Markets

Israel is a shopper's paradise with a wide range of options for those looking for traditional souks and markets to modern malls and designer boutiques. If you're looking to experience the traditional shopping culture in Israel, then you should definitely visit the souks and markets.

One of the most popular markets in Israel is the Carmel Market in Tel Aviv. The market is a great place to buy fresh fruits, vegetables, nuts, and spices. The market is also home to many street food stalls serving delicious local delicacies like falafel, hummus, and shakshuka.

The Mahane Yehuda Market in Jerusalem is another popular market that is worth visiting. The market is known for its fresh produce, baked goods, and Middle Eastern spices. The market also has many cafes and restaurants where you can relax and enjoy a cup of coffee or a meal.

In addition to the traditional souks and markets, Israel also has many modern malls and shopping centers. The Azrieli Center in Tel Aviv is one of the largest shopping centers in Israel with over 180 stores. The center is home to many international brands like Zara, H&M, and Mango, as well as Israeli designers.

The Malha Mall in Jerusalem is another popular shopping destination. The mall has over 200 stores and is home to many international brands like Nike, Adidas, and Calvin Klein, as well as many Israeli designers.

If you're looking for designer boutiques, then you should definitely visit the Rothschild Boulevard in Tel Aviv. The boulevard is home to many high-end fashion boutiques like Louis Vuitton, Gucci, and Prada, as well as many Israeli designers.

Israel is also known for its jewelry, and there are many shops and markets where you can find beautiful handmade jewelry. The Old City of Jerusalem is a great place to buy jewelry, as there are many shops selling traditional Middle Eastern jewelry.

When shopping in Israel, it's important to remember to bargain. Bargaining is a common practice in the markets and souks, and you can often get a better price if you're willing to negotiate.

It's also important to note that most stores and markets in Israel are closed on Shabbat, which is from Friday evening to Saturday evening. Some stores and markets may also close early on Friday.

In terms of payment, most stores and markets in Israel accept credit cards, but it's always a good idea to have some cash on hand, especially when shopping in the markets and souks.

Overall, shopping in Israel is a fun and unique experience, with a wide range of options for every budget and style. Whether you're looking for traditional souks and markets or modern malls and designer boutiques, Israel has something for everyone.

Modern Shopping Malls and Boutiques

In addition to traditional markets and souks, Israel also has a variety of modern shopping malls and boutique shops to satisfy any shopping cravings. Here are some of the best shopping destinations in Israel:

1. Dizengoff Center (Tel Aviv): This is one of Tel Aviv's largest and oldest shopping malls, with over 400 stores offering a range of clothing, shoes, electronics, and more.
2. Mamilla Mall (Jerusalem): This outdoor mall is located near the Old City of Jerusalem and boasts a variety of high-end stores, restaurants, and cafes.
3. Azrieli Center (Tel Aviv): This modern complex houses three towers, with a shopping mall at its base that includes over 180 stores, a food court, and a movie theater.
4. Carmel Market (Tel Aviv): This bustling market in the heart of Tel Aviv offers a wide range of fresh produce, meats, cheeses, spices, and other culinary delights.

5. Nachalat Binyamin Market (Tel Aviv): This outdoor market takes place every Tuesday and Friday and features over 200 artists and craftspeople selling unique handmade items.

6. Shenkin Street (Tel Aviv): This trendy street in the heart of Tel Aviv is lined with boutique shops selling fashion, jewelry, and home decor.

7. Grand Canyon (Haifa): This shopping mall in Haifa features over 200 stores, a food court, and a movie theater, all surrounded by beautiful gardens and water features.

8. Hatachana (Tel Aviv): This restored train station in Tel Aviv has been transformed into a trendy shopping and entertainment complex, with shops, restaurants, and bars housed in historic buildings.

9. Sarona Market (Tel Aviv): This indoor food market in Tel Aviv features over 90 vendors selling a variety of

international and local cuisine, as well as artisanal products and gifts.

10. Levinsky Market (Tel Aviv): This market in the Florentin neighborhood of Tel Aviv offers a unique selection of spices, dried fruits, nuts, and other Middle Eastern treats.

Overall, Israel offers a diverse range of shopping experiences, from traditional markets and souks to modern shopping malls and boutiques. Whether you're looking for unique handmade items or high-end fashion, there's something for everyone in Israel.

CHAPTER 18:   NIGHTLIFE   IN ISRAEL

As a visitor to Israel, there are many exciting nightlife options to explore. Here are some popular options:

1. Tel Aviv: Tel Aviv is known for its lively nightlife scene, with a wide variety of bars, clubs, and music venues. The city has a reputation for being liberal and progressive, and many of its nightlife establishments reflect this vibe. Some popular areas for nightlife in Tel Aviv include the Rothschild Boulevard area, the Shuk HaCarmel market, and the Florentin neighborhood.

2. Jerusalem: Jerusalem is a more conservative city than Tel Aviv, but it still has a nightlife scene worth exploring. There are many bars and restaurants in the city center that stay open late, as well as a few clubs and music venues. The Mahane Yehuda

market is also a popular spot for nightlife in Jerusalem, with many bars and restaurants in the area.

3. Haifa: Haifa is a port city in northern Israel that has a growing nightlife scene. There are several bars and clubs in the downtown area, as well as a few music venues. The city also hosts several festivals throughout the year that feature live music and other cultural events.

4. Eilat: Eilat is a resort town on the Red Sea that is known for its warm weather and beautiful beaches. The town also has a lively nightlife scene, with many bars and clubs catering to tourists and locals alike. Some popular nightlife spots in Eilat include the Ice Mall, which features an ice skating rink and several bars, and the Red Sea Jazz Festival, which takes place every summer.

Overall, Israel has a diverse and exciting nightlife scene that is worth exploring. Just be aware that some establishments may have dress codes or other restrictions, so it's always a good idea to check ahead of time.

Bars, Clubs, And Music Venues

Israel has a wide variety of bars, clubs, and music venues catering to all tastes. Here are some popular options:

1. Tel Aviv:
- The Block: A popular nightclub that features electronic music and hosts international DJs.
- The Pasaz: A club with a retro vibe, playing mostly indie and rock music.
- Kuli Alma: A bar and club that hosts live music, DJs, and art exhibitions.
- Alphabet: A trendy rooftop bar with a great view of the city, serving cocktails and snacks.
2. Jerusalem:
- The Yellow Submarine: A live music venue that hosts local and international acts in a variety of genres.
- Video Pub: A popular bar that screens music videos and hosts live music and DJ events.

- Hataklit: A club that plays mostly Middle Eastern and Arabic music, with a lively atmosphere.
3. Haifa:
- Mushroom Club: A nightclub that hosts electronic music and live performances.
- Zappa Haifa: A live music venue that hosts local and international acts in a variety of genres.
- Underground: A small club with a laid-back vibe, playing mostly indie and rock music.
4. Eilat:
- 5 Monkey's: A popular bar with a beachy atmosphere, serving cocktails and playing music.
- Three Monkeys: A bar and club that hosts live music and DJ events, with a dance floor and outdoor seating.
- Barvaz: A bar and club with a Middle Eastern vibe, playing mostly Arabic and Israeli music.

Overall, Israel has a lively and diverse nightlife scene, with something for everyone. Keep in mind that opening hours and dress codes may vary depending on the establishment, so it's always a good idea to check ahead of time.

LGBT-Friendly Nightlife Options

Israel is generally considered to be one of the most LGBT-friendly countries in the Middle East, and many bars, clubs, and music venues in the country cater specifically to the LGBT community. Here are some popular options:

1. Tel Aviv:

- Shpagat: A bar and club with a mixed crowd and a focus on LGBT-friendly events.
- Evita: A long-standing LGBT-friendly club with drag shows, DJs, and a lively atmosphere.
- Anna Loulou Bar: A bar with a Middle Eastern vibe, serving cocktails and hosting live music and other events.
2. Jerusalem:
- Video Pub: A popular bar that screens music videos and hosts LGBT-friendly events.
- The Toy Bar: A mixed bar with a friendly atmosphere and regular LGBT-friendly events.
3. Haifa:
- Beit Hapsanter: A bar and music venue with a focus on indie and alternative music, hosting regular LGBT-friendly events.
- Barvaz: A bar and club with a Middle Eastern vibe, known for its

LGBT-friendly atmosphere and events.

Overall, Israel has a reputation for being a safe and welcoming destination for LGBT travelers, and many establishments throughout the country are specifically geared towards the LGBT community.

CHAPTER 19: ISRAELI INNOVATION AND TECHNOLOGY

Israel is known for its innovative and entrepreneurial spirit, and the country has developed a thriving technology industry over the past few decades. Here are some examples of Israeli innovation and technology:

1. Cybersecurity: Israel is a world leader in cybersecurity, with many of the world's top cybersecurity companies based in the country. Some notable examples include Check Point, CyberArk, and Palo Alto Networks.
2. Startups: Israel has one of the highest concentrations of startups in the world, with many successful companies emerging from the country's vibrant tech ecosystem. Some notable examples include Waze, Mobileye, and Fiverr.
3. Agriculture: Israel has developed innovative agricultural technologies

that have helped to increase crop yields and conserve water resources. Some notable examples include drip irrigation, which allows farmers to water crops more efficiently, and aquaponics, which combines aquaculture and hydroponics to grow crops using less water.

4. Medical technology: Israel has developed many innovative medical technologies, including pill cameras that can be swallowed to diagnose digestive disorders, and robotic surgical systems that can perform complex procedures with greater precision.

5. Space technology: Israel has developed a growing space industry, with the country's first astronaut, Ilan Ramon, traveling to space in 2003. Israel has also developed a number of satellites and space-related technologies, including the Beresheet

spacecraft, which reached the moon in 2019.

Overall, Israel's innovation and technology industry is a key driver of the country's economy and a source of pride for its people.

Start-Up Culture and Tech Hubs

Israel has a vibrant start-up culture and is home to several thriving tech hubs. Here are some examples:

1. Tel Aviv: Tel Aviv is often referred to as the "Start-up City," and is home to many successful tech companies and start-ups. The city is known for its lively tech ecosystem, with co-working spaces, accelerators, and networking events taking place regularly.
2. Herzliya: Herzliya is another major tech hub in Israel, with many international tech companies setting up offices in the city. The area is home

to several innovation centers, research institutes, and start-up accelerators.

3. Haifa: Haifa is known for its research and development industry, and is home to several major tech companies, including IBM and Intel. The city is also home to the Technion, one of Israel's top engineering schools.

4. Beer Sheva: Beer Sheva is emerging as a major tech hub in southern Israel, with the opening of the Advanced Technologies Park in 2015. The park is home to several major tech companies, as well as a cyber security research center.

5. Jerusalem: Jerusalem has a growing start-up culture, with several accelerators and co-working spaces catering to tech entrepreneurs. The city is also home to the Hebrew University of Jerusalem, which has a strong focus on research and innovation.

Overall, Israel's start-up culture and tech hubs are a testament to the country's innovative spirit and entrepreneurial mindset. The government has also been supportive of the tech industry, providing funding and resources to help start-ups grow and succeed.

Hi-Tech Tours and Experiences

If you're interested in experiencing Israel's hi-tech industry firsthand, there are several tours and experiences you can take part in. Here are some examples:

1. Startup Nation Central: Startup Nation Central is a non-profit organization that connects businesses and investors with Israel's tech ecosystem. The organization offers guided tours of Tel Aviv's tech scene, giving visitors the opportunity to meet with start-up founders and learn about the latest innovations.

2. Microsoft Israel Innovation Center: Microsoft has a research and development center in Herzliya, which offers tours and hands-on experiences for visitors. The center showcases the latest technology from Microsoft, including augmented reality and artificial intelligence.

3. Intel Museum: Intel has a museum in Haifa, which offers guided tours of the company's research and development center. Visitors can learn about the latest advances in computing technology, and see some of Intel's latest products in action.

4. CyberGym: CyberGym is a cyber security training center in Hadera, which offers immersive experiences for visitors. Participants can learn about the latest cyber security threats and how to defend against them, through interactive simulations and training exercises.

5. WeWork Labs: WeWork has several co-working spaces and start-up incubators in Tel Aviv, which offer tours and events for visitors. WeWork Labs provides resources and support for start-ups, and visitors can learn about the latest innovations from some of Israel's most promising entrepreneurs.

Overall, Israel offers many opportunities to experience its hi-tech industry, whether through guided tours or hands-on experiences. These tours can provide a unique insight into the country's innovative spirit and entrepreneurial mindset.

Innovation and Entrepreneurship Conferences

Israel is home to several innovation and entrepreneurship conferences that bring together entrepreneurs, investors, and experts from around the world. Here are some examples:

1. DLD Tel Aviv Innovation Festival: The DLD Tel Aviv Innovation Festival is an annual event that showcases Israel's tech ecosystem and brings together entrepreneurs, investors, and industry leaders. The festival includes conferences, networking events, and startup competitions.
2. OurCrowd Global Investor Summit: OurCrowd is a Jerusalem-based crowdfunding platform for startups, and the OurCrowd Global Investor Summit is an annual event that brings together investors and entrepreneurs from around the world. The event includes keynote speakers, panels, and startup pitches.
3. VivaTech: VivaTech is a major technology conference held in Paris, which features startups, investors, and industry leaders from around the world. Israel is typically well-represented at the conference,

with many Israeli startups showcasing their latest innovations.

4. Cyber Week: Cyber Week is an annual cyber security conference held at Tel Aviv University, which attracts experts from around the world. The conference features keynote speakers, panels, and workshops on the latest cyber security threats and technologies.

5. Innovate Israel: Innovate Israel is a conference and expo that showcases Israel's technology and innovation ecosystem. The event features keynote speakers, panels, and startup pitches, as well as exhibitions of the latest technologies and innovations.

Overall, these conferences provide opportunities for entrepreneurs and investors to network, learn about the latest innovations, and connect with industry leaders from around the world.

CHAPTER 20:   ITINERARIES

Israel has a lot to offer visitors, from its rich history and cultural heritage to its modern cities and hi-tech industry. Here are some itinerary ideas for exploring the country:

1. Highlights of Israel: This itinerary covers some of Israel's most popular destinations, including Jerusalem, Tel Aviv, the Dead Sea, and Masada. Visitors can explore the Old City of Jerusalem, experience the vibrant nightlife of Tel Aviv, and relax in the healing waters of the Dead Sea.
2. Biblical Israel: For those interested in religious history, this itinerary includes visits to several biblical sites, including Nazareth, Bethlehem, the Sea of Galilee, and Jerusalem. Visitors can explore the places where Jesus lived and preached, and learn about the history of Christianity and Judaism.

3. Desert Adventure: This itinerary takes visitors to the Negev Desert, where they can explore the stunning landscapes of this remote region. Activities include hiking in the desert, visiting Bedouin communities, and experiencing the unique culture of this part of Israel.

4. Food and Wine Tour: Israel has a vibrant culinary scene, with a mix of traditional Middle Eastern cuisine and modern fusion dishes. This itinerary includes visits to food markets, vineyards, and restaurants, where visitors can sample some of Israel's best dishes and wines.

5. Hi-Tech Tour: For those interested in Israel's thriving tech industry, this itinerary includes visits to tech hubs in Tel Aviv, Haifa, and other cities. Visitors can learn about the latest innovations in cyber security, artificial intelligence, and other cutting-edge technologies.

These are just a few itinerary ideas for exploring Israel. With its diverse landscapes, rich history, and thriving modern culture, there is something for everyone to enjoy.

Suggested Itineraries for Different Lengths of Stay and Interests, Including Options for Solo Travelers, Families, And Couples.

Israel is a fascinating and diverse country that offers a wealth of cultural, historical, and natural attractions for travelers of all ages and interests. Whether you're a solo traveler looking for adventure, a family seeking fun and relaxation, or a couple seeking romance and culture, Israel has something for everyone. With its mix of ancient ruins, modern cities, stunning landscapes, and religious sites, Israel is a destination that should be on every traveler's bucket list.

To help you plan your trip to Israel, we have put together some suggested itineraries for different lengths of stay and interests. From short weekend getaways to longer trips, these itineraries will help you make the most of your time in Israel.

1. **Two-day itinerary for solo travelers**

If you're a solo traveler with limited time, this two-day itinerary will give you a taste of Israel's vibrant culture and history.

Day 1: Tel Aviv

Start your day in Tel Aviv, Israel's cosmopolitan hub, with a walk along the seaside promenade. Stop at the Carmel Market, one of the largest open-air markets in Israel, to sample some of the local cuisine and buy some souvenirs.

In the afternoon, visit the Tel Aviv Museum of Art to see works by Israeli and international artists. End your day by taking in a show at the Habima Theatre, Israel's national theater.

Day 2: Jerusalem

Take an early morning bus or train to Jerusalem, Israel's ancient capital. Spend the day exploring the city's historical and religious sites, including the Western Wall, the Church of the Holy Sepulchre, and the Dome of the Rock.

Take a stroll through the Old City's narrow streets and alleys, and visit the colorful bazaars and shops. End your day with a sunset view from the Mount of Olives.

2. Three-day itinerary for families

If you're traveling with your family, this three-day itinerary will give you a taste of Israel's family-friendly attractions and activities.

Day 1: Tel Aviv

Spend your first day in Tel Aviv exploring the city's family-friendly attractions. Visit the Tel Aviv Port, a bustling entertainment and shopping complex with restaurants, cafes, and boutiques. Take a stroll through the nearby Hayarkon Park, Israel's largest urban park, with its playgrounds, bike paths, and gardens.

In the afternoon, visit the Children's Museum, where kids can learn and play through interactive exhibits and workshops.

Day 2: Dead Sea and Masada

Take a day trip to the Dead Sea, the lowest place on earth, and Masada, an ancient fortress built by King Herod. Float in the salty waters of the Dead Sea, known for their therapeutic properties, and hike up Masada's steep cliffs for stunning views of the surrounding desert.

Day 3: Jerusalem

Spend your last day in Jerusalem exploring the city's family-friendly attractions. Visit the Israel Museum, which features a collection of ancient and modern art and artifacts, and the Biblical Zoo, home to a wide variety of animals mentioned in the Bible.

Take a stroll through the German Colony, a picturesque neighborhood with cafes, shops, and restaurants, and enjoy a picnic in the nearby Sacher Park.

3. **Five-day itinerary for couples**

If you're traveling with your significant other, this five-day itinerary will give you a taste of Israel's romantic and cultural attractions.

Day 1: Tel Aviv

Start your trip in Tel Aviv, Israel's most cosmopolitan city. Stroll along the beach promenade, explore the Old Jaffa Port, and enjoy a romantic dinner at one of the city's many restaurants.

Day 2: Caesarea and Haifa

Take a day trip to Caesarea, an ancient Roman city on the Mediterranean coast, and Ha ifa, a beautiful coastal city with stunning gardens and a rich cultural heritage. Visit the Caesarea National Park, where you can explore the ruins of the ancient city, including a Roman amphitheater and a Crusader fortress. In Haifa, visit the Baha'i Gardens, a UNESCO World Heritage Site with stunning terraces and panoramic views of the city and the sea.

Day 3: Jerusalem

Take a day trip to Jerusalem, Israel's ancient capital, and explore the city's cultural and religious sites. Visit the Old City's narrow streets and alleys, and explore its many bazaars, shops, and restaurants. Visit the Western Wall, the Church of the Holy

Sepulchre, and the Dome of the Rock, three of the world's most important religious sites.

Day 4: Dead Sea and Ein Gedi

Take a day trip to the Dead Sea and Ein Gedi, a beautiful oasis in the Judean Desert. Float in the salty waters of the Dead Sea, known for their therapeutic properties, and enjoy a relaxing day at one of the many spas and resorts along the shore. In Ein Gedi, hike in the beautiful nature reserve and enjoy the stunning waterfalls and natural pools.

Day 5: Tel Aviv

Spend your last day in Tel Aviv exploring the city's art and culture scene. Visit the Tel Aviv Museum of Art, which features works by Israeli and international artists, and the Bauhaus Center, which showcases the city's unique Bauhaus architecture. Enjoy a romantic sunset view from the rooftop bar of one of the city's many hotels or restaurants.

4. Seven-day itinerary for history and culture enthusiasts

If you're a history and culture enthusiast, this seven-day itinerary will take you on a journey through Israel's rich past and present.

Day 1: Tel Aviv

Start your trip in Tel Aviv, Israel's cultural and artistic hub. Visit the Tel Aviv Museum of Art and the Bauhaus Center, which showcase the city's unique architectural and artistic heritage. Enjoy a stroll along the beach promenade and a romantic dinner at one of the city's many restaurants.

Day 2: Jaffa and Caesarea

Visit the ancient port city of Jaffa, which dates back to biblical times and is known for its beautiful alleys, markets, and artists' studios. From Jaffa, take a day trip to Caesarea, an ancient Roman city on the

Mediterranean coast, and explore its ruins and museums.

Day 3: Jerusalem

Take a day trip to Jerusalem, Israel's ancient capital and a city sacred to three major world religions. Visit the Old City's historical and religious sites, including the Western Wall, the Church of the Holy Sepulchre, and the Dome of the Rock. Explore the city's many bazaars, shops, and restaurants, and enjoy a romantic dinner at one of its many fine dining establishments.

Day 4: Masada and Dead Sea

Visit Masada, an ancient fortress built by King Herod, and hike up its steep cliffs for stunning views of the surrounding desert. From Masada, continue to the Dead Sea, the lowest place on earth, and float in its salty waters, known for their therapeutic properties. Spend the night at one of the many luxurious resorts and spas along the shore.

Day 5: Galilee

Take a day trip to the Galilee region, a beautiful area with rolling hills, vineyards, and ancient towns. Visit the Sea of Galilee, where Jesus is said to have walked on water, and explore the many historical and religious sites in the region, including the Mount of Beatitudes, the ancient city of Tiberias, and the Capernaum synagogue.

Day 6: Tel Aviv

Spend your last full day in Tel Aviv exploring the city's vibrant contemporary culture scene. Visit the Tel Aviv Museum of Contemporary Art, which features works by Israeli and international artists, and explore the city's many galleries, street art, and music venues. Enjoy a romantic dinner at one of the city's many trendy restaurants or rooftop bars.

Day 7: Negev Desert

Take a day trip to the Negev Desert, a vast and stunning wilderness area in southern Israel. Explore the beautiful natural landscapes, including canyons, cliffs, and sand dunes, and visit the ancient Nabatean city of Avdat, a UNESCO World Heritage Site. End your trip with a romantic dinner under the stars at one of the desert's many luxury camps and lodges.

5. Ten-day itinerary for families

If you're traveling with your family, this ten-day itinerary will take you on a fun and exciting journey through Israel's many attractions for kids and adults alike.

Days 1-3: Tel Aviv

Start your trip in Tel Aviv, where you can enjoy the city's many beaches, parks, museums, and family-friendly attractions. Visit the Tel Aviv Port, which features a boardwalk, a market, and many restaurants and cafes. Take a stroll in Park HaYarkon, one of the city's largest and most beautiful parks, and visit the Zoological Center of Tel Aviv-Ramat Gan, a popular attraction for kids and adults alike.

Days 4-5: Jerusalem

Take a day trip to Jerusalem and explore the city's many historical and religious sites, including the Western Wall, the Church of the Holy Sepulchre, and the Dome of the Rock. Visit the Tower of David Museum, which tells the story of the city's rich history, and enjoy a family-friendly evening show at the City of David.

Days 6-7: Galilee

Visit the Galilee region, a beautiful area with rolling hills, vineyards, and ancient towns. Visit the Sea of Galilee and enjoy a family-friendly boat ride, visit the Hula Valley Nature Reserve, which is home to many species of birds and animals, and explore the ancient city of Tiberias.

Days 8-9: Dead Sea and Ein Gedi

Visit the Dead Sea, where you and your family can float in the salty waters and enjoy a day at one of the many family-friendly resorts and spas along the shore. From the Dead Sea, continue to Ein Gedi, a beautiful oasis in the Judean Desert, where you can hike in the nature reserve and enjoy the stunning waterfalls and natural pools.

Day 10: Tel Aviv

Spend your last day in Tel Aviv enjoying the city's family-friendly attractions, including the Luna Park amusement park, the Tel Aviv Port, and the Museum of the Jewish People. End your trip with a family-friendly dinner at one of the city's many restaurants.

6. Ten-day itinerary for couples

If you're traveling with your significant other, this ten-day itinerary will take you on a romantic journey through Israel's many attractions for couples.

Days 1-2: Tel Aviv

Start your trip in Tel Aviv, where you can enjoy the city's beaches, parks, museums, and vibrant nightlife. Take a stroll in Park HaYarkon, one of the city's largest and most beautiful parks, and visit the Tel Aviv Museum of Art, which features works by Israeli and international artists. Enjoy a romantic dinner at one of the city's many fine dining establishments, or a drink at one of its rooftop bars.

Days 3-4: Jaffa and Caesarea

Visit the ancient port city of Jaffa, which dates back to biblical times and is known for its beautiful alleys, markets, and artists' studios. From Jaffa, continue to Caesarea, a beautiful coastal city with a rich history. Visit the ancient Roman amphitheater, the Crusader fortress, and the city's beautiful beaches.

Days 5-6: Jerusalem

Take a day trip to Jerusalem and explore the city's many historical and religious sites, including the Western Wall, the Church of the Holy Sepulchre, and the Dome of the Rock. Visit the Tower of David Museum, which tells the story of the city's rich history, and enjoy a romantic evening stroll in the Old City's narrow alleys and hidden courtyards.

Days 7-8: Galilee

Visit the Galilee region, a beautiful area with rolling hills, vineyards, and ancient towns. Take a romantic boat ride on the Sea of Galilee, visit the Hula Valley Nature Reserve, which is home to many species of birds and animals, and explore the ancient city of Tiberias. Enjoy a romantic dinner at one of the region's many fine restaurants, which feature local wines and fresh produce.

Days 9-10: Dead Sea and Ein Gedi

Visit the Dead Sea, where you and your partner can float in the salty waters and enjoy a day at one of the many luxury resorts and spas along the shore. From the

Dead Sea, continue to Ein Gedi, a beautiful oasis in the Judean Desert, where you can hike in the nature reserve and enjoy the stunning waterfalls and natural pools. End your trip with a romantic dinner under the stars at one of the desert's many luxury camps and lodges.

Israel offers a diverse range of attractions and activities for travelers of all ages and interests. Whether you're a solo traveler looking to explore the country's rich history and culture, a family seeking fun and adventure, or a couple in search of romance and relaxation, Israel has something for everyone. These suggested itineraries are just a starting point, and travelers are encouraged to tailor their trips to their own interests and preferences. With its rich history, stunning natural landscapes, and vibrant culture, Israel is a destination that should not be missed.

Social Opportunities for Solo Travelers

As a solo traveler in Israel, there are plenty of opportunities to socialize and meet new people. Here are some suggestions for social opportunities in Israel:

1. Join a tour group: Israel is a popular destination for group tours, and there are plenty of tour companies that cater to solo travelers. Joining a group tour is a great way to meet other travelers and explore the country together.
2. Stay in a hostel: Hostels are a popular accommodation option for solo travelers, and many hostels in Israel offer social events and activities for guests, such as pub crawls, group dinners, and city tours.
3. Participate in a volunteer program: There are many volunteer opportunities in Israel, from community service projects to archaeological digs. Participating in a

volunteer program is a great way to meet locals and other volunteers who share your interests.

4. Take a cooking class: Israeli cuisine is known for its unique flavors and influences from around the world. Taking a cooking class is a fun way to learn about Israeli culture and meet other food enthusiasts.

5. Attend a cultural festival: Israel is home to many cultural festivals throughout the year, from music festivals to film festivals to religious celebrations. Attending a festival is a great way to experience Israeli culture and meet locals and other travelers who share your interests.

6. Join a hiking or adventure group: Israel is a great destination for outdoor enthusiasts, with many opportunities for hiking, cycling, and other adventure activities. Joining a hiking or adventure group is a great way to meet other like-minded

travelers and explore the country's natural beauty.

7. Visit a language exchange meetup: If you're interested in learning Hebrew or practicing your language skills, there are many language exchange meetups in Israel where you can meet locals and other language learners.

Overall, Israel offers many opportunities for solo travelers to socialize and meet new people. Whether you're interested in culture, food, adventure, or language learning, there is something for everyone in Israel.

Solo Travel Resources and Communities

There are many resources and communities available for solo travel in Israel. Here are some suggestions:

1. Solo Traveler World: Solo Traveler World is an online community of solo travelers from around the world. They have a forum where travelers can connect with each other, ask questions, and share their experiences. They also have a Facebook page where they share articles, tips, and travel inspiration.
2. Israel Ministry of Tourism: The Israel Ministry of Tourism website provides a wealth of information on solo travel in Israel, including recommended itineraries, safety tips, and information on local events and attractions.
3. Israel Travel Forum: The Israel Travel Forum is an online community where

travelers can ask questions and get advice from other travelers who have been to Israel. The forum covers a wide range of topics, including solo travel, accommodation, and transportation.

4. Hostels in Israel: Hostels in Israel are a great option for solo travelers on a budget. They offer affordable accommodation and are a great place to meet other travelers. Hostelworld.com is a good resource for finding hostels in Israel.

5. Tours and activities: Joining a tour or activity can be a great way to meet other travelers and explore Israel safely. There are many companies that offer tours and activities in Israel, including G Adventures and Intrepid Travel.

6. Couchsurfing: Couchsurfing is a community of travelers who offer free accommodation to other travelers. It's a great way to meet locals and get a

unique perspective on the destination. The Couchsurfing website also has a section for meetups, where travelers can connect with each other in person.

CHAPTER 21: ISRAEL'S NEIGHBORING COUNTRIES

Israel is located in the Middle East and shares borders with several neighboring countries. While some of these countries may not have the best diplomatic relationships with Israel, they are still popular destinations for travelers visiting the region. Here are some of Israel's neighboring countries that visitors may be interested in:

1. Jordan: Located to the east of Israel, Jordan is a popular destination for visitors looking to explore the ancient city of Petra, the Wadi Rum desert, and the Dead Sea. Visitors can also experience traditional Bedouin culture, enjoy Jordanian cuisine, and visit historical sites such as Jerash.

2. Egypt: To the southwest of Israel, Egypt is home to world-famous historical sites such as the pyramids of Giza, the Sphinx, and Luxor. Visitors

can also explore the bustling capital city of Cairo, cruise along the Nile River, and relax on the beaches of the Red Sea.

3. Lebanon: To the north of Israel, Lebanon offers a unique blend of Middle Eastern and Mediterranean culture. Visitors can explore the cosmopolitan capital city of Beirut, hike in the scenic Lebanese mountains, and visit historical sites such as the ancient city of Byblos.

4. Syria: While travel to Syria is currently not recommended due to ongoing conflict, before the war, visitors could explore the ancient city of Damascus, visit the ruins of Palmyra, and experience Syrian cuisine and culture.

5. The Palestinian Territories: Located within Israel's borders, the Palestinian Territories include the West Bank and Gaza Strip. Visitors can explore the ancient city of Bethlehem, visit historical sites such as the Church of

the Nativity and the Dome of the Rock, and learn about the Palestinian-Israeli conflict.

It is important to note that travel to some of these neighboring countries may require additional documentation, such as visas or permits, and visitors should check the latest travel advisories and guidelines before planning their trip.

Day Trips and Excursions to Nearby Countries

1. Petra, Jordan: Petra is a UNESCO World Heritage site located in southern Jordan, about a 3-hour drive from Eilat, Israel. It is famous for its ancient rock-cut architecture, including the Treasury, Monastery, and Great Temple. Visitors can take a day trip from Eilat to Petra, where they can explore the site with a local guide.

2. Cairo, Egypt: Cairo is the capital city of Egypt, located about a 1-hour flight from Tel Aviv, Israel. Visitors can take a day trip to Cairo to explore the Pyramids of Giza, the Sphinx, the Egyptian Museum, and the Khan El Khalili Bazaar.

3. Dead Sea, Jordan: The Dead Sea is a unique natural wonder located on the border between Israel and Jordan. Visitors can take a day trip from Jerusalem to the Jordanian side of the Dead Sea, where they can float in the salty waters, enjoy mud treatments, and relax in the luxurious spas.

4. Beirut, Lebanon: Beirut is the capital city of Lebanon, located about a 1-hour flight from Tel Aviv, Israel. Visitors can take a day trip to Beirut to explore the city's rich history and culture, including the National Museum, the Pigeon Rocks, and the Mohammad Al-Amin Mosque.

5. Ramallah, Palestine: Ramallah is the administrative capital of the Palestinian Territories, located just a short distance from Jerusalem. Visitors can take a day trip to Ramallah to explore the city's vibrant cultural scene, including the Yasser Arafat Museum, the Dar Zahran Heritage Building, and the Al-Manara Square.

As with any international travel, it is important to check the latest travel advisories and guidelines before planning a day trip or excursion to a nearby country from Israel.

Cross-Border Travel Logistics and Considerations

Cross-border travel between Israel and its neighboring countries can be complicated, and there are several logistics and considerations to keep in mind before planning a trip. Here are some important things to consider:

1. Visa requirements: Visitors should check the visa requirements for each country they plan to visit. Some countries may require a visa or permit, while others may allow visa-free travel or issue visas on arrival. It is important to obtain the necessary documentation before traveling.

2. Border crossings: Visitors should be aware of the border crossings between Israel and its neighboring countries. Some crossings may have restricted access or limited hours of operation, and visitors should plan their travel accordingly. It is also important to check the latest border crossing information and to follow any security measures in place.

3. Health and safety: Visitors should be aware of any health and safety concerns in the countries they plan to visit. Some areas may be prone to

political instability, violence, or natural disasters, and visitors should stay informed and take necessary precautions.

4. Currency exchange: Visitors should be aware of the currency exchange rates and availability of local currency in the countries they plan to visit. It is recommended to exchange currency at official exchange offices or banks to avoid scams or counterfeit money.

5. Language: Visitors should be prepared for language barriers in the countries they plan to visit. While English is widely spoken in many tourist areas, it is helpful to learn some basic phrases in the local language to facilitate communication and show respect for the local culture.

It is important to stay informed and updated on the latest travel advisories and guidelines before planning a cross-border trip from Israel. Visitors should also consider working with a reputable travel agency or tour operator to help with logistics and ensure a safe and enjoyable travel experience.

Cultural and Historical Connections with Neighboring Countries

Israel shares many cultural and historical connections with its neighboring countries due to its location at the crossroads of the Middle East. Here are some of the notable cultural and historical connections between Israel and its neighboring countries:

1. Jordan: Jordan and Israel share a common history, particularly in the region of the Jordan River Valley. Both countries also have a significant population of Palestinians, which has led to cultural exchanges and shared traditions.
2. Egypt: Egypt and Israel share a long history, dating back to ancient times when the Pharaohs ruled over the region. The two countries also share cultural and religious connections,

particularly with regards to the story of the Exodus and the Jewish Passover holiday.

3. Lebanon: Lebanon and Israel share a complex and often contentious history, with conflict and political tensions overshadowing cultural connections. However, both countries have a shared Mediterranean culture, and many Lebanese and Israeli citizens share similar traditions and customs.

4. Palestine: Palestine and Israel share a long and complicated history, with shared religious and cultural connections that date back thousands of years. Both populations have deep roots in the region, and the conflict between the two groups has shaped the cultural and political landscape of the area.

5. Syria: Syria and Israel share a complex and often hostile history, with the two countries being involved in multiple

conflicts over the years. However, both countries share a rich history and culture, particularly with regards to the ancient city of Damascus and the many religious sites located throughout the region.

Despite the political tensions and conflicts between Israel and its neighboring countries, there are many cultural and historical connections that link these nations together. Visitors to the region can explore these connections through cultural tours, historic sites, and museums, gaining a deeper understanding of the complex history and culture of the Middle East.

CHAPTER 22: HAUNTED AND SUPERNATURAL SITES

There are some places in Israel that are believed to have supernatural or haunted significance based on local folklore and legends. Here are some examples:

1. The Tower of David - The Tower of David is an ancient citadel located in Jerusalem's Old City. According to local legends, the tower is haunted by the ghost of a woman who was falsely accused of adultery and executed. Visitors have reported hearing her screams and footsteps in the tower's dark corridors.

2. The Cave of Machpelah - The Cave of Machpelah is a burial site located in Hebron, believed to be the resting place of the biblical patriarchs and matriarchs. According to Jewish tradition, the spirits of the deceased still inhabit the site, and visitors have

reported hearing whispers and footsteps in the cave's chambers.

3. The Red Sea - According to local Bedouin folklore, the Red Sea is home to a supernatural creature known as the djinn. The djinn are believed to be powerful spirits that can take on human or animal forms and have been known to lure unsuspecting travelers to their deaths.

4. The Church of the Holy Sepulchre - The Church of the Holy Sepulchre is one of the holiest sites in Christianity, believed to be the site of Jesus' crucifixion, burial, and resurrection. Visitors have reported experiencing supernatural phenomena such as sudden temperature drops, unexplained noises, and strange apparitions while visiting the church.

5. The Western Wall - The Western Wall is a sacred site in Judaism, believed to be the last remaining remnant of the Second Temple. According to Jewish

tradition, the wall is a place where prayers are answered, and visitors have reported experiencing supernatural phenomena such as hearing voices, feeling sudden bursts of energy, and seeing apparitions while praying at the wall.

Again, it is important to note that these are just local legends and folklore, and there is no scientific evidence to support the existence of supernatural or haunted places. Visitors to these sites should always show respect for the cultural and religious significance of the places they visit.

Ghost Tours and Paranormal Experiences

There are several ghost tours and paranormal experiences available in Israel. Here are some options:

1. The Jerusalem Ghost Tour - This tour takes you through the Old City of Jerusalem, where you will hear stories

of ghosts, haunted buildings, and other supernatural phenomena. You'll visit places like the Tower of David, the Old Jewish Quarter, and the Church of the Holy Sepulchre.

2. Haunted Safed Tour - Safed is a city in northern Israel that is known for its mystical traditions. This tour takes you through the city's old alleys and cemeteries, where you'll hear stories of ghosts, haunted buildings, and other paranormal experiences.

3. Acre's Haunted Underground Tour - Acre is a coastal city in northern Israel that has a long and rich history. This tour takes you through the city's underground tunnels and dungeons, where you'll learn about the city's dark past and hear stories of ghosts and supernatural occurrences.

4. The Dead Sea Paranormal Experience - The Dead Sea is a unique natural wonder that is said to have healing properties. This experience takes you

to the Dead Sea to witness and participate in a paranormal ritual that is said to cleanse the mind and body.

5. The Golan Heights UFO Tour - The Golan Heights is a mountainous region in northern Israel that has been the site of many UFO sightings over the years. This tour takes you to the best vantage points for viewing UFOs and tells the stories of some of the most famous sightings in the area.

Please note that some of these tours and experiences may not be suitable for all ages or may have limited availability. It's always a good idea to check with the tour operator before booking to make sure it's a good fit for you.

CHAPTER 23: PRACTICAL INFORMATION

Here are some practical information about Israel that might be helpful for travelers:

1. Currency - The currency in Israel is the Israeli shekel (ILS). You can exchange foreign currency at banks and exchange offices throughout the country.
2. Language - The official languages of Israel are Hebrew and Arabic. However, many Israelis speak English as well, especially in tourist areas.
3. Transportation - Israel has a well-developed transportation system, including buses, trains, and taxis. You can also rent a car, but keep in mind that driving in Israel can be challenging due to heavy traffic and aggressive driving.
4. Weather - Israel has a Mediterranean climate, with hot, dry summers and mild, rainy winters. Be sure to pack

accordingly and stay hydrated during the hot summer months.

5. Safety - Israel is generally a safe country to travel in, but it's always a good idea to take common-sense precautions, especially in crowded areas or tourist spots. Be aware of your surroundings, keep an eye on your belongings, and follow local guidelines and advice.

6. Electricity - The standard voltage in Israel is 220 volts, with a frequency of 50 hertz. The power outlets are Type H, which is unique to Israel and has three flat prongs. If you're traveling from a country with a different type of plug, you'll need an adapter.

I hope this information is helpful for your travels in Israel!

Passport and Visa Requirements

Passport Requirements:

- All visitors to Israel must have a valid passport.
- The passport must be valid for at least six months beyond the date of entry.
- Make sure your passport has enough blank pages for entry and exit stamps.

Visa Requirements:

- Visitors from many countries can enter Israel without a visa for up to 90 days. This includes citizens of the United States, Canada, the European Union, Australia, and New Zealand, among others.
- Citizens of some countries, including China, Russia, and India, require a visa to enter Israel.
- If you're unsure whether you need a visa, you can check with the Israeli embassy or consulate in your home country.

For those who need a visa:

- Tourist visas can be obtained at Israeli embassies and consulates abroad before arrival.
- Some nationalities can apply for a visa upon arrival at the airport or border crossing, but it's always best to confirm this with the embassy or consulate beforehand.
- Business visas and work permits require additional documentation and processing.

It's important to note that visa requirements are subject to change, so it's always a good idea to check the latest information with the Israeli embassy or consulate in your home country before you travel.

Communication options (e.g. Wi-Fi, SIM cards, phone plans)

Here are some communication options for travelers in Israel:

Wi-Fi:

- Wi-Fi is widely available in Israel, especially in hotels, cafes, and restaurants.
- Many tourist attractions also offer free Wi-Fi, such as museums and parks.
- Some cities also have public Wi-Fi networks that you can connect to for free, such as the "FreeWiFi" network in Tel Aviv.

SIM Cards and Phone Plans:

- If you have an unlocked phone, you can purchase a SIM card from a local provider and sign up for a phone plan.
- The main cellular providers in Israel are Cellcom, Pelephone, and Partner.
- You can purchase a SIM card at the airport or at a cellular provider store throughout the country.
- Prepaid plans are available, and you can usually add data, voice, and text packages to suit your needs.

- Some plans may also include international calling and texting options.

Important note:

- To purchase a SIM card in Israel, you'll need to present your passport and have your phone unlocked.
- If you don't have an unlocked phone, you can rent a phone or purchase a cheap phone and SIM card package.
- International roaming can be expensive, so using a local SIM card can be a more affordable option.

I hope this information helps you stay connected during your travels in Israel!

Tips for A Successful and Enjoyable Trip

Here are some tips for a successful and enjoyable trip to Israel:

1. Plan ahead - Research the places you want to visit, the things you want to do, and the best time to go. Make sure you have all necessary travel documents and reservations in advance.
2. Be respectful - Israel is a religious and culturally diverse country, so it's important to be respectful of local customs and traditions. Dress modestly when visiting religious sites, and be aware of cultural differences.
3. Stay hydrated - Israel can get hot, especially in the summer months. Make sure you stay hydrated by drinking plenty of water and avoiding sugary drinks and alcohol.
4. Try the local food - Israel has a diverse culinary scene, with influences from Jewish, Arabic, and Mediterranean cuisine. Don't be afraid to try new foods and flavors!
5. Stay safe - Israel is generally a safe country, but it's always important to

take precautions when traveling. Be aware of your surroundings, keep your belongings close, and follow local safety guidelines.

6. Use public transportation - Israel has a well-developed transportation system, including buses, trains, and taxis. Using public transportation can be a convenient and affordable way to get around.

7. Learn some Hebrew - While many Israelis speak English, learning a few Hebrew phrases can go a long way in making connections with locals and experiencing the culture.

8. Embrace the history - Israel is a country with a rich history and many important historical sites. Take time to visit these sites and learn about the country's past.

9. Take time to relax - While there's plenty to see and do in Israel, it's also important to take time to relax and recharge. Spend a day at the beach,

enjoy a spa treatment, or take a leisurely stroll through a park.

I hope these tips help you have a successful and enjoyable trip to Israel!

Respecting The Local Culture and Environment

Respecting the local culture and environment is an important part of being a responsible traveler. Here are some tips for doing so during your trip to Israel:

1. Dress appropriately - Israel is a religious and culturally diverse country, so it's important to dress modestly when visiting religious sites and in more conservative areas. Avoid wearing revealing clothing, and cover your shoulders and knees when appropriate.
2. Respect religious customs - Israel is home to many different religions, including Judaism, Christianity, and Islam. Be respectful of local religious

customs, such as removing your shoes before entering a mosque or wearing a head covering when visiting a synagogue.

3. Learn about local customs - Take the time to learn about local customs and traditions, such as the Sabbath, which begins on Friday evening and ends on Saturday evening. Be aware of cultural differences and be respectful of them.

4. Support local businesses - Supporting local businesses is a great way to contribute to the local economy and culture. Shop at local markets, eat at local restaurants, and stay in locally owned accommodations.

5. Reduce your environmental impact - Israel is home to many beautiful natural areas, including beaches, parks, and nature reserves. Be mindful of your environmental impact by not littering, conserving water, and using eco-friendly products when possible.

6. Be mindful of sensitive political topics - Israel is a politically sensitive country, and discussions of politics can be heated. Be respectful of different viewpoints, and avoid sensitive political topics when possible.

7. Learn a few words of Hebrew or Arabic - Learning a few words of Hebrew or Arabic can go a long way in showing respect for local culture and making connections with locals.

By following these tips, you can help to respect the local culture and environment during your trip to Israel.

Common Scams to Avoid

While Israel is a safe country to travel to, it's always important to be aware of common scams that can occur in tourist areas. Here are some common scams to avoid:

1. Fake taxis - Be wary of unlicensed taxis, especially those that offer to take you to your destination for a lower price. Always make sure the taxi has a meter and that the driver is licensed.
2. Overcharging - Be aware of overcharging at restaurants, shops, and markets. Always check the price of items and services before making a purchase, and be prepared to negotiate.
3. Street vendors - Street vendors can be pushy and may try to sell you overpriced or fake goods. Be cautious when approached by street vendors and avoid buying from them unless you are confident in the quality of the goods.
4. Pickpocketing - Pickpocketing can occur in crowded tourist areas, such as markets and public transportation. Keep your valuables close to your body and be aware of your surroundings.

5. Charity scams - Be wary of charity scams that ask for donations or offer to sell you goods to support a charitable cause. Always research the organization before making a donation or purchase.
6. ATM scams - Be cautious when using ATMs, as skimming devices and cameras can be used to steal your card information. Always cover the keypad when entering your PIN and use ATMs in well-lit, secure areas.

By being aware of these common scams, you can avoid falling victim to them and enjoy a safe and enjoyable trip to Israel.

Dealing with Unexpected Situations

Even with the best planning, unexpected situations can still arise while traveling. Here are some tips for dealing with unexpected situations during your trip to Israel:

1. Stay calm - It's important to stay calm in unexpected situations. Take a deep breath and try to assess the situation before taking action.
2. Seek help - If you need assistance, don't be afraid to ask for help. Contact your hotel or the local authorities for assistance.
3. Have emergency numbers on hand - Make sure you have emergency numbers on hand, such as the local police, ambulance, and fire department. Keep these numbers in a safe and accessible place.
4. Keep important documents safe - Keep your passport, travel insurance documents, and other important documents in a safe and secure place. Consider making copies of these documents and keeping them in a separate location.
5. Be prepared for medical emergencies - Make sure you have travel health insurance and bring any necessary

medication with you. Know the location of the nearest hospital or medical center in case of a medical emergency.

6. Have a backup plan - It's always a good idea to have a backup plan in case of unexpected situations. For example, have an alternative itinerary in case a site you planned to visit is closed.

7. Stay informed - Keep up-to-date with local news and weather reports to be aware of any potential risks or hazards.

8. Follow local guidelines and regulations - During times of political or social unrest, there may be restrictions or guidelines in place for your safety. Stay informed of any local guidelines or regulations and follow them to avoid any issues or conflicts.

Remember that unexpected situations can happen, but with a bit of preparation and a calm and rational approach, you can overcome them and continue to enjoy your trip to Israel.

Israeli Slang and Colloquialisms

Israeli slang and colloquialisms can be difficult to understand for those who are not familiar with them. Here are some common ones:

1. Sababa (סַבָּבָּה) - This means "cool" or "great." It's often used to express agreement or enthusiasm.
2. Yalla (יָאלְלָה) - This is a popular expression that means "let's go" or "come on." It can also be used to encourage someone to hurry up.
3. Balagan (בַּלְגָן) - This word means "mess" or "chaos." It can be used to describe a situation that is out of control.
4. Chutzpah (חֻצְפָּה) - This is a Hebrew word that means "nerve" or "audacity." It's often used to describe someone who is bold or impudent.

5. Tachles (תַּכְלִית) - This word means "bottom line" or "essence." It's often used to cut through the small talk and get to the point.

6. Slichah (סְלִיחָה) - This word means "sorry" or "excuse me." It's a polite way to apologize or ask for someone's attention.

7. Shalom (שָׁלוֹם) - This word means "peace" or "hello." It's a common greeting in Hebrew and is often used as a farewell as well.

8. Achla (אַחְלָה) - This means "awesome" or "amazing." It's a popular slang word used to express enthusiasm or excitement.

9. Mizrachit (מִזְרָחִית) - This word means "eastern" and is often used to describe people or things that have a Middle Eastern or Arabic influence.

10. Chaval al hazman (חָבַל עַל הַזְּמַן) - This phrase means "a waste of time" and is often used to express frustration or disappointment.

Hebrew Survival Phrases for Travelers

Here are some Hebrew survival phrases that may be useful for travelers:

1. Shalom (שָׁלוֹם) - Hello/Goodbye
2. Toda (תּוֹדָה) - Thank you
3. Boker tov (בּוֹקֶר טוֹב) - Good morning
4. Erev tov (עֶרֶב טוֹב) - Good evening
5. Ken (כֵּן) - Yes
6. Lo (לֹא) - No
7. Bevakasha (בְּבַקָּשָׁה) - Please
8. Slicha (סְלִיחָה) - Excuse me/Sorry
9. Ani lo medaber/medaberet Ivrit (אֲנִי לֹא מְדַבֵּר/ת עִבְרִית) - I don't speak Hebrew (masculine/feminine)
10. Mah ze oseh? (מַה זֶה עוֹשֶׂה?) - What is this?
11. Kama ze oleh? (כַּמָּה זֶה עוֹלֶה?) - How much does this cost?
12. Ein li ben chorin (אֵין לִי בֶּן חוֹרִין) - I don't have free time

13. Ani mevaksha map (אֲנִי מְבַקֵּשׁ מַפָּה) - Can I have a map please?

14. Yesh po mi she-medaber Anglit? (יֵשׁ פּוֹ מִי שֶׁמְדַבֵּר אַנְגְּלִית?) - Is there anyone here who speaks English?

15. Todah rabah, lehitraot! (תּוֹדָה רַבָּה, לְהִתְרָאוֹת) - Thank you very much, goodbye!

16. Here are some Hebrew survival phrases that may be useful for travelers:

17. Shalom (שָׁלוֹם) - Hello/Goodbye

18. Toda (תּוֹדָה) - Thank you

19. Boker tov (בּוֹקֶר טוֹב) - Good morning

20. Erev tov (עֶרֶב טוֹב) - Good evening

21. Ken (כֵּן) - Yes

22. Lo (לֹא) - No

23. Bevakasha (בְּבַקָּשָׁה) - Please

24. Slicha (סְלִיחָה) - Excuse me/Sorry

25. Ani lo medaber/medaberet Ivrit (אֲנִי לֹא מְדַבֵּר/ת עִבְרִית) - I don't speak Hebrew (masculine/feminine)

26. Mah ze oseh? (מַה זֶּה עוֹשֶׂה?) - What is this?

27. Kama ze oleh? (?כַּמָּה זֶה עוֹלֶה) - How much does this cost?

28. Ein li ben chorin (אֵין לִי בֶּן חוֹרִין) - I don't have free time

29. Ani mevaksha map (אֲנִי מְבַקֵּשׁ מַפָּה) - Can I have a map please?

30. Yesh po mi she-medaber Anglit? (יֶשׁ פֹּה מִי שֶׁמְדַבֵּר אַנְגְלִית?) - Is there anyone here who speaks English?

31. Todah rabah, lehitraot! (תּוֹדָה רַבָּה, לְהִתְרָאוֹת) - Thank you very much, goodbye!

Making The Most of Your Trip

Here are some tips for making the most of your trip:

1. Plan ahead: Research the places you want to visit, make a rough itinerary, and book accommodations and tours in advance.

2. Be flexible: While it's good to have a plan, don't be too rigid with your itinerary. Allow some flexibility to explore unexpected opportunities or to adjust your plans based on weather or other factors.

3. Take your time: Don't try to cram too many activities into your trip. Allow yourself plenty of time to really experience each place you visit and immerse yourself in the local culture.

4. Connect with locals: Meeting and talking with locals can give you a deeper understanding of the local culture and can lead to new experiences and opportunities.

5. Try local cuisine: Eating local food is one of the best ways to experience a new culture. Try street food, local specialties, and regional dishes to get a taste of the local flavors.

6. Get off the beaten path: While popular tourist attractions are worth visiting, don't be afraid to explore less crowded

areas. Some of the best experiences can be found in lesser-known towns, neighborhoods, or parks.

7. Learn about the history and culture: Learning about the history and culture of a place can enrich your travel experience. Read books, visit museums, and talk to locals to learn more about the place you're visiting.

8. Take care of yourself: Travel can be tiring, so it's important to take care of yourself. Get plenty of rest, stay hydrated, and eat healthy food. Don't forget to take breaks and relax when you need to.

9. Keep a travel journal: Writing down your experiences can help you remember the details of your trip and reflect on what you've learned and experienced.

10. Be respectful: Show respect for the local culture and traditions, including dress codes, religious customs, and local norms. Be mindful of the impact

of your actions on the local environment and community.

11. Take photos: Photos are a great way to capture memories of your trip. Take plenty of photos, but also take time to enjoy the moment without a camera in your hand.

12. Try something new: Travel is a great opportunity to try new things. Try a new activity, food, or language to step out of your comfort zone and broaden your horizons.

13. Stay safe: While traveling, it's important to take basic safety precautions. Be aware of your surroundings, avoid dangerous areas, and keep your valuables safe.

14. Have fun: Most importantly, have fun! Travel is about experiencing new things and enjoying yourself. Embrace the adventure and make the most of your trip.

Final Thoughts and Next Steps

As you prepare to embark on your journey to Israel, there are many final thoughts and next steps that you should keep in mind to ensure that your trip is enjoyable, safe, and memorable.

First and foremost, it's important to remember that Israel is a country with a complex history and a diverse population. It is a land that is holy to three major religions, and as such, it is steeped in culture and tradition. When traveling to Israel, it's important to approach the country with an open mind and a willingness to learn and explore.

One of the best ways to fully experience Israel is to plan your trip ahead of time. Israel is a relatively small country, but it's packed with a variety of attractions and activities, from ancient historical sites to modern cultural attractions. Researching these attractions and making a rough itinerary will help you make the most of your time in Israel and ensure that you don't miss any must-see destinations.

It's also important to be flexible with your itinerary. While it's great to have a plan, be open to unexpected opportunities that may arise during your trip. Israel is a country that is full of surprises, and sometimes the most memorable experiences come from going off the beaten path and exploring new areas.

When traveling to Israel, one of the most rewarding experiences is connecting with locals. Israelis are known for their hospitality and friendliness, and making an effort to connect with them can lead to incredible experiences and insights into the local culture. Whether it's striking up a conversation with a vendor at a market or meeting locals through an organized tour, connecting with Israelis is a great way to get a deeper understanding of the country and its people.

Trying local cuisine is also a must when traveling to Israel. Israeli food is a unique blend of Mediterranean and Middle Eastern flavors, with dishes that range from the classic hummus and falafel to modern fusion cuisine. Eating street food and regional specialties is a great way to immerse yourself in the local culture and get a taste of the local flavors.

As you explore Israel, take the time to learn about the history and culture of the places you visit. Israel is a country with a rich history, and learning about its past can give you a deeper appreciation for its present. Whether it's visiting ancient historical sites or exploring modern museums, there are many opportunities to learn and expand your knowledge of the country.

Staying safe is also a top priority when traveling to Israel. While the country is generally safe for tourists, it's important to take basic safety precautions, such as being aware of your surroundings, avoiding dangerous areas, and keeping your valuables safe. Additionally, it's important to respect the local customs and traditions, including dress codes and religious customs.

Finally, remember to have fun! Travel is all about experiencing new things and making memories that will last a lifetime. Embrace the adventure and make the most of your time in Israel.

As for next steps, there are many resources available to help you plan your trip to Israel. Travel websites and blogs can provide you with up-to-date information on the best places to visit, while guidebooks can give you a comprehensive overview of the country and its attractions. Additionally, travel agents can help you plan your trip and make bookings for accommodations, tours, and transportation.

In terms of practical considerations, it's important to make sure that you have all the necessary documents and vaccinations before traveling to Israel. Ensure that your passport is valid for at least six months beyond your intended stay, and consider getting travel insurance to protect against unexpected events.

Finally, don't forget to pack appropriately for your trip. Israel has a Mediterranean climate, with hot summers and mild winters, so be sure to pack clothing that is appropriate for the season. Additionally, comfortable walking shoes are a must for exploring the many historical sites and attractions that Israel has to offer.

Most Frequently Asked Questions and Answers About Visiting Israel

Here are some frequently asked questions and answers about visiting Israel:

1. Is Israel safe for tourists?

Yes, Israel is generally safe for tourists. The country has a well-developed security infrastructure and a low crime rate, and tourism is a key part of the country's economy. However, it is important to take basic safety precautions, such as being aware of your surroundings and avoiding dangerous areas.

2. What is the best time of year to visit Israel?

The best time to visit Israel depends on your preferences and the activities you plan to do. The summer months (June-August) are hot and crowded, while the winter months (December-February) are mild and rainy. Spring (March-May) and fall (September-November) are generally considered the best times to visit, with mild weather and fewer crowds.

3. What should I wear when visiting Israel?

Israel is a religious country, and modest dress is expected in many areas. It is generally recommended to dress conservatively and cover your shoulders, knees, and chest when visiting religious sites or attending formal events. Additionally, it's a good idea to pack comfortable walking shoes, as there are many historical sites and attractions that require walking.

4. What are the must-see attractions in Israel?

Israel has many must-see attractions, including the Old City of Jerusalem, the Dead Sea, Masada, Tel Aviv's beaches, the Sea of Galilee, and the ancient city of Caesarea. Additionally, there are many museums, art galleries, and cultural attractions throughout the country.

5. What is the currency used in Israel?

The currency used in Israel is the Israeli shekel (ILS). Most major credit cards are widely accepted, and there are many ATMs throughout the country. It's a good idea to inform your bank of your travel plans before leaving, to avoid any issues with accessing your funds.

6. What language is spoken in Israel?

The official language of Israel is Hebrew, but English is widely spoken throughout the country. Additionally, Arabic is spoken by the Arab minority in Israel.

7. Can I visit the West Bank and Gaza Strip?

Visiting the West Bank and Gaza Strip is possible, but it is important to check the current political situation before traveling. Visitors should also be aware that entry into the Palestinian territories may require special permits or visas.

8. How do I get around in Israel?

Israel has a well-developed transportation system that includes buses, trains, and taxis. Public transportation is affordable and convenient, and many hotels and tourist areas offer shuttle services to popular attractions. Taxis are readily available in most areas, but it's important to negotiate the fare before getting into the cab.

9. What are the food and drink options in Israel?

Israel has a diverse and vibrant culinary scene, with a mix of Mediterranean and Middle Eastern flavors. Must-try dishes include hummus, falafel, shakshuka, and Israeli salad. Additionally, there are many local wines and craft beers to sample.

10.   Do I need a visa to visit Israel?

Citizens of many countries, including the United States, Canada, and most of Europe, do not need a visa to enter Israel for stays of up to 90 days. However, it's a good idea to check the current visa requirements before traveling.

11. Is it easy to find vegetarian and kosher food in Israel?

Yes, Israel has many options for vegetarian and kosher food. Most restaurants offer vegetarian options, and many traditional dishes are vegetarian or can be modified to be vegetarian. Additionally, there are many restaurants that are certified kosher, and it's easy to find kosher food in most areas.

12. What should I know about the religious customs and traditions in Israel?

Israel is a religiously diverse country, with Judaism, Christianity, and Islam being the major religions. It's important to be respectful of the religious customs and traditions, especially when visiting religious sites. For example, it's customary to dress modestly and cover your head when visiting Jewish religious sites, and to remove your shoes when visiting mosques.

13. Can I use my phone and internet in Israel?

Yes, most major phone carriers offer international plans that include coverage in Israel. Additionally, there are many Wi-Fi hotspots throughout the country, and most hotels and cafes offer free Wi-Fi.

14. What should I do if I need medical assistance while in Israel?

Israel has a well-developed healthcare system, and there are many hospitals and medical facilities throughout the country. If you need medical assistance, seek help from a medical professional or visit the nearest hospital or medical clinic. It's also a good idea to have travel insurance that covers medical emergencies.

15. Are there any cultural events or festivals in Israel that I should attend?

Yes, Israel has many cultural events and festivals throughout the year, including the Jerusalem Film Festival, the Tel Aviv Gay Pride Parade, and the Festival of Lights in Jerusalem. Additionally, there are many music and dance festivals, as well as cultural events that celebrate the country's diverse history and traditions.

Israel is a fascinating and beautiful country with a rich history and culture. From the religious sites in Jerusalem to the beaches of Tel Aviv, there is something for everyone to enjoy. By taking the time to plan ahead and do some research, you can make the most of your trip and have an unforgettable experience in Israel.

Made in United States
Orlando, FL
03 January 2025

56801202R00225